Colour The Cosmic Code

This book is based on *the truth* as I see it today.

What *my truth* will be tomorrow, is unknown.

Who knows to what and to where one's imagination will lead me.

The *truth* goes as far as you can stretch your imagination.

Your imagination is your link to:

The Cosmos and The Light.

GOD.

A BOOK ON COLOUR

by Antony J. Cooper 1999

Published by Unicorn 2000/Aura Light,
Rainbow Farm, Buckland Rd,
Bampton. Oxen. OX182AA

© Antony J. Cooper 1999

First printing September 1999

National Library of Australia
ISBN 0 646 33468 9

Dedication

I would like to dedicate this book to Marion for her unending support and ability to keep me on track in my many endeavours, to my daughters Shiralee and Tina for their love and understanding in so many ways within this lifetime.

To George, Vicky, Simon, Vince, Marcel, and Gurudas for their inspirational paths to follow, as well as all the many Souls incarnate and discarnate who in so many ways have shared my Rainbow Dream, this time round...

Colour the Cosmic Code

This book includes information which is in part practical in nature covering what can be easily digested by any interested person, through to a more sophisticated blue print and outline for the professional's use and application, then forward to an area of more complexity for the Visionary, providing ground breaking philosophical and conceptual foundations which encourage access to the Cosmic Inter-dimensional spectrum of networks and advanced grid-works connecting many energy levels from the sub atomic Microcosm, to the Mega dimensional Macrocosm. This is the time to facilitate assimilation of deeper levels of understanding and development by mankind to support the great leap forward, the quantum leap.

Contents

Contents

About the Author

Tony Cooper's journey through life has been one painted in a richly coloured palette. His quest to self-understanding has been an interesting trail with footsteps keen to follow the path less taken.

My father, Tony Cooper was born in London, England in 1934 and moved with his family to the island of Jersey in 1954. In 1967 he and Marion migrated with their young family to Australia.

This search to unveil the source of life has been touched by the lives of many others who have likewise opened the curtain. Meeting like minds empowers us to break from programmed restrictions, thankfully my parents were always considered different. Dad was drawn into the healing arts even before I was born. Crystals adorned our home well before it became fashionable. People from all walks of life and religions shared our welcome mat.

Whilst working behind the shop front, Tony began questioning the secrets of life. This intent grew stronger as Tony discovered through his interior decorating in the 70's that there was more to colour than meets the eye. Books on Colour Psychology started to find their way into the home.

Tony left interior decorating but he kept within his heart the need to know more about this infinite energy. Many years of hard work was rewarded in time by the opportunity to follow the dream.

Eventually in 1988 Tony and Marion ventured to England where they met Vicky Wall. This meeting cemented the dream. Upon their return to Australia, Vince

Halpin suddenly reappeared with his amazing insight into vibrational medicine. Tony and Marion Cooper later established Aura Light in 1991 at Unicornis in Mapleton, Queensland. The home of Colour Harmonics was born.

Sharing this cosmic code became Tony's life purpose. Tony has been invited to speak to numerous groups worldwide over the past 10 years. Their lecturing tours have included Australia, Canada, Denmark, England, France, Germany, Japan, New Zealand, Scotland, Singapore, and the United States. Sharing the podium with doctors and psychologists, Tony has gained respect for his understanding of colour as a tool for re mem ber ing. This knowledge is based upon a lifetime of experience.

Tony's conviction to share a more colourful world has inspired him to spend many hours with a not so friendly computer as his companion. This work gives access to his profound understanding of colour to all who wish to share his vision of light.

Tony and Marion now live in the idyllic village of Bampton on the edge of the Cotswolds in England. Rainbow Farm is their centre for teaching as well as the production and distribution of their Unicorn 2000/Aura Light products. The Australian base is run by Shiralee Cooper at Unicornis, Mapleton.

Light has bestowed to us all the gift of colour. Tony Cooper is one who wishes to share this cherished gift. This is a book for all who wish to understand the language of this cosmic code!

Introduction

And then there was light…

Light has bestowed upon us the gift of colour. Both light and colour are essential to our existence. My journey has inspired me to explore and share this cosmic code with all who dare to follow the rainbow bridge to self discovery.

Colour plays a very important psychological and often symbolic part within our daily lives shaping our inner and outer worlds. Colour arouses strong feelings and emotions within mankind by having such a powerful direct influence upon our thinking and feeling processes, creating anything from aggression to tranquillity. Colour and its uses as far as the human mind is concerned, is inexhaustible and never ending. The practice of using colour as a healing agent has been known and practised for many thousands of years by civilisations of bygone days which had a much better understanding of colour knowledge than most people have today. Ancient colour therapies covered the treatment of many illnesses and diseases. Clearly it has been practised in the temples of ancient Egypt and Greece spanning back in excess of four thousand years.

Colour is a subjective experience for the artist, as well as the viewer or observer, leading many people through history to explore and analyse not only colour but art and the artist's use of this medium. Scientists, biologists, psychologists and many other illustrious people of the past and present have all discussed and formulated the phenomena of colour.

Colour is not only recorded by the eye but is also perceived by the mind, suggesting that colour remains constant to the mind regardless of illumination. Artists have learnt to manipulate colour, resulting in a perceived illumination, creating an illusion of fixed or projected colour.

Colour has the power to act dynamically upon our imaginations. Fixed colours give objects specific energy responses to the viewer, but any object having a reflective surface seems to have a life of its own, always being able to change and respond to any ambient light source whilst still influencing the soul through the mind. This has inspired many Spiritualists and Theosophists such as Madam Blavatsky who wrote at length of her experiences with the phenomena between colour and soul.

Charles Leadbeater found that the relationship of the three primary colours did link to specific shapes. He came to this conclusion through a survey which asked many people to correspond certain colours with specific shapes. (not including the platonic solids)? He concluded that Red linked to squares, Yellow to triangles, and Blue to circles.

Freud found a relationship of colour to mankind, but so too did certain abstract and surrealist artists whilst trying to record dreams and visions from a subconscious level, relating colour to form. This recognition of colour's relationship to one's multiple levels of being reveals the language of the Cosmic Code. Colour within healing wasn't re-discovered until the beginning of the 20th century, when once again the subject was taken seriously. Even then, it was looked upon as something akin to the occult, having rather mystical and even spiritual values.

Most information as to the potential of Colour Therapy was passed on by small groups, sects and even secret societies. This research continued through the study of art in its many forms, the subtle understanding of the old masters, even now not really comprehended. We do know that this or that artist went through their blue period or their orange period. This I believe had more to do with their mental and emotional states using the colours they needed themselves to express themselves. A good example is Van Gogh's Sunflowers, the predominant colour being orange, which indicates deep emotional turmoil.

Some fragments of this past knowledge are reflected within our present day language. These have been passed down to us from past civilisations, not always being our own. These phrases are in everyday use even now. Just feeling off colour is rather an interesting comment. We wisely say, *you should show your true colours* without realising the true meaning as with *seeing red, feeling green with envy* or *feeling blue, the scarlet woman* and *the red light district*. There are many more and it is hard to recognise how many colour coded references there are in our modern English language.

Today colour is being recognised as the cornerstone of psychology with increasing evidence showing our inner understanding of the relationship between every colour and shade to each altered state of our physical well being.

Colours are linked to events and circumstances within our lives, as well as relating to past, present and even the future events. Colour is a wonderful tool to move beyond the barriers of consciousness and to explore the truth's of being.

The presence of light and colour is accepted by most people of the world today as being just a matter of course. Yet if we were cut off from light, our world would quickly become extinct. Whether we realise it or not, light and therefore colour, has a major dominance upon and within our lives. From the time of awakening in the morning until we retire in the evening, we are saturated by an ever-changing relationship with those colours that are presented to you and which we perceive on so many different levels of our consciousness. We are today so used to this kaleidoscope of colour from our childhood to our grave, it becomes so familiar and as the saying goes, "Familiarity breeds contempt." We just seem to take it all for granted.

The invisible rays of light with their unseen energy transform into each respective colour according to the reflective qualities of the surfaces of objects and elements. These reflected vibrational frequencies are de-coded by the eye and then passed to the brain which then creates the images and sensations that are transmitted to our outer levels of being. Colour mainly works in conjunction with the eye, brain, and thinking/feeling systems, triggering a bewildering array of responses, some conscious whilst many others are sub-conscious.

Application of colour to the body works mainly in conjunction with our body's subtle energy system, through to our multiple levels of consciousness within each and every cell. Yes colour talks to us on a cellular level giving new or renewed energy patterns for the cells to energise and harmonise. Once enough of our cells consciousness has been re-patterned or changed, this information is then transferred to our physical body and conscious levels of being, which is then used to change the creative consciousness. When this re-patterned change in consciousness has been made, a resulting new relationship of harmony between your thinking and your feelings can come about, leading to body harmony and good health. Colour is gradually being used once again for healing the sick in mind, body and spirit. The full potential for healing and the release of destructive creative programs from our systems is yet to be realised.

I personally believe that in the future, colour linked together with other forms of vibrational medicine will be in common use to treat illnesses and will prove to be a most powerful tool in preventative medicine. Colour holds very important keys to future knowledge of the self on all levels, leading us directly to the cause of any present disharmony. Unfortunately this seems so far removed from what is happening today. People in the main are trying to heal symptoms, not their causes. Colour is leading the way to the future of preventative medicine, getting to the cause of any imbalance within our physical and mental systems before it becomes a major problem.

Bringing colour into our daily lives helps in connecting with the corresponding different facets of one's Self. Colour is the visual impulse that inspires us to realise our inner richness. It is the most powerful catalyst and motivator, helping us to recognise our Universality which is firmly imbedded within our consciousness and to remember [re-member = put together] our true Selves. These colour seeds within grow into action to help our lives unfold and if understood, blossom into a fuller and richer life in so many ways.

Colour is symbolically and visually evocative,

being of ancient lineage and yet contemporary,

profound but easy to use.

Colour helps us to frequently remember our infinite nature allowing us to claim the universe within and leading us to recognise that we are indeed the God of our own personal Universe.

Unicorn 2000/Aura Light is a way of using colour to explore and to know yourself more fully and in so doing, we come to realise that inner universe that lies within us all, that great treasure house of images and knowledge. Colour holds the keys to the way in and it holds the codes to our inner mind locks, thus opening up to us the purpose of our being, our destiny, our life's purpose. We were born to grow in consciousness, which of course means, to Know Yourself. An awareness of colour is the conceptual basis for the Unicorn 2000/Aura Light self-diagnostic system of Harmony Bottles.

The Cosmic Code has been given as a gift to mankind. With wisdom and intelligence seeded within, the order in which these keys are presented is an exact numerical sequence. We can only advance physically by consciously moving forward and using our thought forms which are in essence the creative connection to the super grids of the cosmic creative source. It is here where the essence of the Light enfolds the cosmic codes once again to be seeded within this time through colour, sound, numbers, and crystalline geometric structures. Through this cosmic language our consciousness is activated to communicate on many new levels, which then can become imbedded within our own levels of reality.

The opening of the higher mind clears and clarifies the many channels to the higher Universal Wisdom of the Seven Seals, Seven colours and the Seven chakras. This wisdom reveals that as we experience all colour, we experience the light, helping us to find our "mastership" and rightful place within the Cosmos. The keys are encoded within colour and other harmonic structures, seeding them with the Living Light split into a new spectrum carrying its hidden alphabet to be released and realised within this dimension thus spelling out mankind's collective birthright. These keys now manifesting, are preparing mankind for the Quantum Leap forward, bringing changes effecting every level of intelligence upon and within this planet. This gives an opportunity for mankind to collectively move into a new system of creation and a new consciousness within the light.

Since the keys have been given together with their teachings to many varied disciplines, making them difficult to be understood by all, the complexity of each key will not be fully recognised at this time. It will take various levels of understanding to know the totality of their encoded planetary intelligence.

The Cosmic Code was created to shape a new creation within the full spectrum of light and Octaves of sound etc., so creating a regenerative harmonious power of biocoupling expressed through colour combinations and each colours geometric blueprint.

These energised combinations are to be used directly onto the body thus re-coding it back to the Light allowing it to consciously experience the direct power of the sacred language and projected thought forms that are held within.

CHAPTER ONE

Colour the Golden Light of the New Age

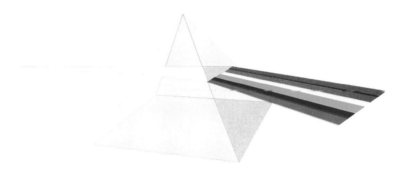

The golden light of this New Age is here and the time is now right for this book on colour and its association with ALCHEMY.

This work contains important information presenting little known facts as well as revealing new understandings and discoveries relating to the interaction of colour with those life flowing energies that control man's health and regeneration processes. Colour is a unique tool for working with our body's energies. *It is a gift of light to enlighten!*

Colour is all pervasive and mostly taken for granted these days, largely unstudied and misunderstood by the majority. Colours affect us on so many levels including our emotional, physical and spiritual levels helping us to feel warm or cool, energised or relaxed whilst reflecting very distinctive effects which are triggered from deep within us Colour thereby enriches our lives through our perception and interaction with it. Can you imagine a colourless world.? Its quite unimaginable! Colour is but a reflection of light enabling us to perceive the constant changes in the world around us, a kaleidoscope of never ending reflections of countless hues.

This colour book can bring to the reader an understanding of the science behind the phenomenon of body and colour interaction. Perhaps somewhere in the past there was a real comprehension of the attuning properties of colour for physical, mental, emotional as well as spiritual healing. Today much of this ancient knowledge is veiled in archaic and esoteric language, blocked by superstition and prejudice, for so long lost to posterity. The here and now is where we can rediscover and explore the use of colour as an instrument of healing on so many different levels of being.

Imagine the human body as a fluctuating field of energy that surrounds and permeates its physical boundaries. This energy field will reveal imbalances in its pattern of flow, your soul's pattern, and your true colours.

Where there are problems within a person's internal organs or related emotional life, habit of thought and being all affect the way energy flows through one's physical body. Disharmony within a person's aura can be balanced, either by passively letting colour do its work, or by attuning one's thoughts to the vibrational frequency of specific colours.

Colour has a beautiful and purposeful mission. Its pristine power of light works on all levels of being. Energy waves from the sun create, sustain and renew life in all the kingdoms on our earth and all the other planes within and around our system. They reflect their vibrationary Rays upon each of these levels. This is the principle that sustains life within our cosmic system and beyond, physically working on the major glandular organs and energy centres of the body.

Negative spots in the health system are visible within one's aura. These are the spots where the soul's light has failed to fully penetrate to the physical, thus not helping to sustain it, but rather lowering one's vitality with a decrease in vibrations, this been the precursor of Decay and Disease.

Mental and emotional behaviour is keyed to the seven major glandular and energy centre's of the physical body as well as another five etheric centres above the head each having a different vibrational frequency from those of the physical chakra system. More on these later.

Mental and emotional stress inhibits the soul's sustaining light and together with ignorance and prejudice blacks out the curtains of one's mental, emotional and spiritual understanding and progress. Through the negation of light, we find that one suffers from physical and nervous ailments and from mental and emotional inversion, perversion and inhibitions amongst other things. Habit, bias, and attitude can produce prolonged lack of nourishing light; light starvation. This impairs the circulation of the life forces to certain parts of the body, resulting in dis-ease.

Emotions create neurochemical effects within our physical body linking our mind to our body, our emotions to our attitudes and to our emotional pain through our bodily symptoms. Thus we can link our physical pain to our lifes' happenings. Either our view is restricted, or the translation of our perceived world to our personal Selves is. We are all locked into or out of our own personal realities or "worlds".

Everyone creates the world that they perceive. It is a world which we believe in according to our programmed perceptions & responses starting from before our very first breath. Our interaction with others is therefore guided through these responses into a world, or worlds of our own creation which include social, economic and belief systems. These intrinsic and extrinsic systems are also very restrictive societal patterns, narrowing our view and perception of all we see. This world we then experience is bought about by many factors and how we experience it is embedded deep within our psyche.

Colour has the ability to reveal the elements of human potential, understanding and the way to accessing information that is hidden deeply with the subconscious levels of being.

As said, this is how Light uses the cosmic language of colour, offering the keys to open human mind locks deep within our levels of consciousness. This information allows an inward journey to freedom. The language of colour is an adventure to discover the higher perceptual level of our true Selves.

Colour transcends the written and spoken word and works within the multi-levels and dimensions of our own perceived reality, according to one's deep seated past recorded experiences. Each and every colour within the known spectrum has a very precise measurable frequency link to specific areas of our physical body, as well as its many energy levels.

Dr. Max Luscher author of the Luscher Test says, "Colour is the mother tongue of the unconscious."* Colours are visible representations of an invisible intangible reality through which our inner world can be revealed to the world outside. The intangible can manifest into something very real indeed.

To understand the meaning of colours, we must attempt to discover the elusive reality which exists behind the tangible, as well as comprehend the links between them. At times this hidden reality or should we say soul of colour, can portray our psychic essence as well as our dreams or potential for the future. (even our longings for change).

An important characteristic of colour is its' transcendent capacity and its' meanings on many levels. When we interpret and ponder the real archetypes behind each colour, we can find their relationships to our physical life, our physical health, wealth and happiness.

Such archetypal patterning and images reflect the typical human circumstances. Our life's transition and direction is also depicted by our choices of colour combinations. These individual archetypal images portrayed by Unicorn 2000, AURA LIGHT's harmony bottles, have provided a constant challenge for me. My experience has inspired this new approach to colour's interrelationships. This has placed these archetypal combinations on a much wider and deeper framework of reference than ever attempted by other colour diagnostic systems.

The possible meanings and understanding of the Unicorn 2000/AURA LIGHT Harmony, diagnostic system takes study of its levels of meaning and their interrelationship with the seeker. It is through the archetypes themselves and our own involvement with them, that we are provided with a new orientation which opens up new levels of consciousness, in turn activating hidden MYSTERIES.

Many people have written about colour in the past, both in ancient and modern times. Generally colour has been dealt with in a very superficial way for such a large and complex subject, usually without showing the importance of colour's relationship to all living organisms. The personal image behind each colour offer new hope of mastering life's challenges. These transformational processes are mirrored by our beautiful colour combinations. When seeking we will only FIND WHATEVER WE ARE PREPARED TO DISCOVER!

It is said that given a choice, we choose what so ever we need and only get what ever we expect.

* Dr Max Luscher...The Luscher Test.

Each and every Cell is a

Being, a unit of life within itself.

Its not just the path we choose…..

But the way we walk that Path.

So let us all "walk our talk".

CHAPTER TWO

Colour is the Key to the Doorway

Stressing colour's importance and the great part it plays within our everyday lives, the Egyptian Papyrus Ebers of 1550 BC wrote about Colour Cures. The early Greeks used tyrian purple for eye problems as well as for a dye for cloth for Kings and Priests. This colour or dye was obtained from a sea snail called Purpura and was also used widely in those days for boils and ulcers. The Chinese and Hindus, as well as the Romans a little later, adhered to the doctrine of The HUMOURS in one form or another. This was a system of colour diagnosis based on a patient's colours such as the skin, eyes and nails as well as their waste products. This system flowed into Western Europe including the United Kingdom during medieval times. Down through the ages great thinkers and teachers such as Plato, Aristotle and Pliny, Pythagoras and Hippocrates each attempted to explain colour's dynamic interaction with humanity. Even Leonardo Da Vinci related colour to the different elements as follows.

Yellow to Earth. **Green to Water. Blue to Air. Red to Fire.**

It is said that Sir Isaac Newton founded in modern terms, the "Science" of colour through the splitting of the spectrum through a prism. The time span of historical memory of colour knowledge had been accepted by many generations until Geothe declared that Newton's colour science was unacceptable, viewed from his era. Now it is our turn to let the Magic of colour work its spell on us and reveal its new face to this generation, recognising that we are now in a different position mentally to understand and accept these new levels of knowledge.

Some one hundred years ago in Great Britain an Association of Colour Therapy was formed which was embraced by the medical practitioners of that time, who frequently prescribed coloured foods and cloths, as well as the use of coloured lights. Today the medical practitioners still use coloured light to cure, as in the use of a blue light for a jaundice premature baby. The babies are placed under this light for two to three days allowing the blue light to penetrate the skin to destroy the excess bilirubin that an immature liver cannot remove. Once the liver is mature enough it is able to cope for itself.

Jung used a colour process of allowing his patients to make spontaneous paintings, a process he called Individuation, which aims at reconciling opposites within oneself. He also found that patients tended to create patterns based on archetypal forms of squares and circles, masculine and feminine forms. Dr Max Luscher based an analysis of personality on an individuals colour preference, revealing and defining "Individuality".

To this day in Australia, Dr Ruth Cilento has used specific mandalas for patients to colour in. Again this is done in a rather spontaneous manner which reveals where they are within their healing process. Colour is the direct link from the subconscious to the conscious. Someone using correct colour knowledge can acquire very specific and important information as to the patient's capacity at any given time to effect a healing in mind, body and spirit.

Dr Ruth Cilento has used the colour knowledge gained from a three year study to create a system that could identify those who wanted to exit this existence. Today Dr Cilento's colour knowledge is found and demonstrated to be very accurate and practical. Very few people today recognise that colour impacts into virtually every realm of human life and culture. There is hardly a single aspect of human progress that has not been affected by colour. Every layman can make colour work for them by paying attention to the use of colour rather than just leaving its choice to chance. Although everything in life has colour, today our choice is mainly the subject of "others'" control.

Colour the key to the door of mysteries

When we talk about different colours we usually mean "HUE" as in hue-man, human.

Are we indeed beings of colour and light?

Although the eye can discern many thousands of different colours of varying hue, saturation and lightness, we have only named a small proportion of these, showing our rather limited colour vocabulary even within our sophisticated languages.

The oldest terms ever found describing colour in every language throughout the known world is always, BLACK and WHITE, roughly translated as dark and light. It follows that our main descriptions of the thousands of hues available to us, are described as, light or dark green, light or dark blue, etc. Many of the more primitive people of the world do not even have these descriptive differences as their word for green may have covered all the hues of green right through to khaki brown.

During the evolution of the English language, many descriptive words have come and gone. In other words, this language is still evolving and doesn't necessarily mean that these primitive people didn't have the ability to perceive the many hues of colour, but rather did not record many descriptive "words" to convey their perception.

Are nature's colours incidental or just chance byproducts of the basic chemistry of life?

The make up of molecules and the arrangement of genes and chromosomes present within the coded nucleus of each and every cell, gives the definition between leaves, flowers and stems and its reflective possibilities.

Colour is the basic structure of evolution exploited by man, plants and animals from the beginning of time.

Spring brings the Green through chlorophyll and later breaks down into the Autumn Red to Yellows, when other pigments are exposed. These colours of nature are used by birds and animals as camouflage or for display and attention seeking.

It was reported that after Mr Gladstone had read Homer's epic Iliad, he thought that the ancient Greeks did not have a clear notion of colours. He concluded that their colour vision was defective, rather than consider that they could possibly lack a descriptive vocabulary. Despite this declaration, Mr Gladstone went on to become the Prime Minister for Great Britain.

Most written work from the past has dealt more with the action and effects of colour rather than naming each hue as we tend to do today. But do we? Even today we only have red and white wine, and some times a little rose. But few come specifically within this colour "labelling".

We do better at labelling horses. We have a large range of descriptive colours, such as Bay, Chestnut, Piebald, Skewbald, Grey, Roan, Strawberry Roan, Dun, Palomino and many others.

As users of so-called sophisticated languages, we seem to require an ever increasing number of descriptive words to allow us to make even more precise colour definitions. We have around 24 basic colour names which we revert to light or dark, even mid colours as well as combination's of two colours. Especially it seems within the blue/violet part of the spectrum ...... Amethyst, Violet, Purple, Magenta, Mauve, Lavender, Lilac, Indigo, Navy Blue, Royal Blue, Prussian Blue, Delph, Marine, Sea, Baby, Sky, Peacock and so many more.

Many, as you can see, are "Look alike" colours, being peacock like or lavender like, and so on. Therefore we need to know the colour of a peacock or the lavender flower to imagine the colour.

As we start to study colour we need to realise the deceptive qualities of colour, for instance a black car always looks smaller than a white or lighter coloured car. A red notice board looks closer than a blue one. By adding stripes or dual tones to a car, it changes its visual shape. Have you noticed that a black suitcase looks heavier than a light coloured one? These deceptive qualities of colour are today used very skilfully by designers of manufactured goods as well as the skilled interior decorator who can change the visual shape of any room or office by colour engineering any internal and external environment for work or pleasure.

It is interesting to note that the same colour hue at different saturations harmonise when displayed together. Complementary colours are harmonious as well as light, medium and dark colours, created simply by adding black (seen in the figure below). The visual size and density of each car seems to differ with each depth of colour.

It is said that red cars go faster, or appear to do so. The illusion is helped by the fact that red appears to be coming toward you and focuses in front of the iris.

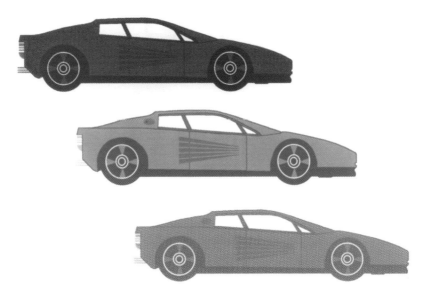

Have a good look at these cars. What does each colour tell you about the car. Which car appears to be larger, heavier, faster etc. Just by colouring each car differently we have given them quite different qualities.

A simple example of colour engineering was when a bus company had a problem getting passengers to move toward the back of the bus, so a designer came up with an ingenious solution. He got the ceiling of the bus painted blue, darker at the front and lighter at the rear and as if by magic, passengers moved themselves naturally to the enlightened end of the bus.

As with the packets and cans within a supermarket, certain colours sell much more readily than others. By using colours, subconscious messages link to our needs and programmed responses to certain colour combinations, and with the colour of price tickets also playing part, goods just fly magically from the shop's shelves into our shopping baskets.

Think about the Yellow ticket with the Red prices upon it which excites us and encourages us to purchase even without checking if the price marked is a "SPECIAL".

This sale type ticket presentation is being used more and more now. Also the colours of RED and YELLOW are the largest selling lines in supermarkets. Check out the multi national companies that use these colours, McDonald's, Burger King, Shell, for example. In fact, the majority are using one or both of these colours, just ask yourself why. Look at the basic structure of these two colours in a later chapter of this book.

Geothe believed colours should be used according to their affect upon the mind. He said that Reds and Yellows were called Plus or Positive colours which give lively, quick and exciting feelings. {Thinking to Feeling Process} He considered the Minus or Negative colours to be from green to blue to violet {blue/red} which he believed gave an impression of Anxious Restlessness. Even from these statements we can start to see a direct link to our physical life and being.

Freudians invariably relate colours back to bodily functions, such as red blood. Freud also believed that his patients ascribed colours to functions of consciousness. i.e. Yellow for intuition, Blue for thinking, Pink for feelings and so on. Today these colour links are quite questionable and in fact many are proven to be completely inaccurate.

Today colour is recognised as an immediate experience, acting directly upon the emotions, abstract in its magical nature with properties it can transfer to any object, anointing it with its transformational qualities. Colours are in fact, forces that directly influence our souls. It has been written many times that colour is to the soul as oxygen is to the body, I agree but see even more benefits.

Many people in the past have written in both a deep or shallow way about the many facets and complexities of colour and their relationships to all living things. People from our ancient past or more recent history have sought to show the importance of colour, together with the part it can and should play in our every day lives. This book is written to back up and maybe re-present little known points of view as well as new revelations. The main objective is to encourage you towards colour knowing. As well I wish to bring you a new approach and understanding of colour as a very accurate diagnostic system.

If we ask where did colour knowledge come from historically, the answer is that it came from everywhere and nowhere. We are born with a sense of colour but could not always understand it enough to use it accurately ...until now.

The language of colour expresses cosmological constants which support both human and higher evolutionary thought forms.

The Primal opposition of Light & Dark, White & Black, Life & Death, gives colour's their ambiguities and qualities and coloured objects their perceived, yet sometimes contradictory associations, qualities and symbolism. For example the saffron robe of the Buddhist Monks adopted so as to represent humility, orange also satisfies the emotional need of the lower gut and their emotional responses. Christian Monks even today use Grey and Black, symbolising renunciation of worldly things, in many countries these colours represent Death and so for example, in many western societies these colours are used as Mourning cloths. Many widow and widowers have used black at times of full mourning, later grey as half mourning after an appropriate length of time has elapsed. This custom can still be seen in use by the Maories in New Zealand, whilst in other countries white or uncoloured cloth is used in mourning.

Mankind in the main has not been able to use the language of colour because humanity has remained under the power of fallen illuminaries (angels).

Aligning themselves with duality, Black & White, mankind has thus been losing their ability to work with other polychromatic (Colour Coded) Realities.

The Language of colour expresses cosmological constants which support both human and higher evolutionary thought forms.

Colour being the language of light, alters the memory substructures of language which affect us on physiological, numerical, biological and cosmological levels of thought attunement, helping to prepare the human mind to embrace the new dimensions of communications now being rediscovered. This attunement has been made available for the present light workers walking this earth to access the universal coding principles which can reprogram man's consciousness to participate in the synchronicity of the many dimensions and time zones of one's super consciousness, harmonising the mind and body with one's higher states of consciousness.

The keys to future breakthrough's in physics, psychology, psychiatry, and medicine will be given through the cross matching of geometric and colour codes. This will allow the structure of the chromosomes and their light/time participating levels of consciousness to be understood.

CHAPTER 3

Colour a Divination Tool
Colour a Universal Tool

Most divination systems are drawn by chance or at random. A choice from a throw of a dice or the turn of a card, purely a blind choice. A random serve of cards face down seems to be very hit or miss one would think, but never the less, many people find "readings" using this method acceptable, allowing the Universe to choose for them.

Unicorn 2000/Aura Light's self diagnostic system through the use of Harmony Bottles is based on our own inner knowledge and knowing of colour, bringing the subconscious to the conscious. The system uses specific ways of choice within strict parameters whilst working closely with the hidden keys to the system which are laid deep within our subconscious. We can then recognise the colour links to our physical, mental, and emotional beings as well as our spiritual Selves and on to our thinking to feeling processes.

The colour keys to the universe....
UNIVERSE = UNI-VERSE = ONE VERSE = ONE SONG.
KEYS = NOTES = MUSIC to the ONE SONG.

If we ask where did colour knowledge come from within a historical point of view, we can mention many names like Pythagoras, Newton, Geothe, Steiner and of course more recently Dr. Max Luscher. But the plain answer is that nobody really knows. More ancient wisdom was passed down orally and much of the written has been translated poorly, sometimes intentionally. In many ways, it's a time of re-discovery, re-aligning, and re-directing colour knowledge into this new age, or this age of re-new-all.

Since my youth the story of colour has exploded.... Colour is no longer just within the reach and province of the privileged and wealthy as in days not so long gone by. Today colour is found in profusion throughout all levels of life and living. It is available in fabrics, metals, plastics, embellishing and enlivening so many diverse manufactured objects and products, from cars to cookers, from cans in the supermarket to the very cloths on our backs.

Colour is enriching our lives on so many different levels, conscious and subconscious, and it is the link to our soul or super conscious levels. As we scan with our eyes, many subtle messages are carried simultaneously to all levels of consciousness and also to each and every cell that forms bodies. These messages feed the cells with information and directions. *We must recognise that every singular cell is a unit of life within itself.*

We are now discovering colour's important potential for healing, understanding and communication and this allows us to understand and bring the full spectrum of colour into our lives. As we can see, colour effects us in so many different ways within every aspect of living. Colour is directed at us through light, especially daylight, showing us the differences between the landscape, sky, and sea, allowing one to differentiate between things such as hair and skin, one flower from another. Nature has a full pallet of colour using the complete spectrum, as do the modern manu-facturers of goods in this day and age creating products for mankind to use and wear.

This access to colour just wasn't available to all mankind even 100 years ago. If one goes further back in history, access was even less available. The colours mankind perceived in those far off days were mainly derived from what nature offered in abundance through plants and berries, bark and leaves and all the other aspects of all that is natural.

Once our consciousness of colour is awakened, this allows one to perceive the myriad of colours given to us through the gift of light. The rose coloured dawns and the crisp blue skies, the crimson sunsets and that great bow in the sky, the rainbow.... all are often so beautiful it is hard to believe one's eyes. Just imagine what Sir Isaac Newton felt when he found that a single droplet of water carried the refractive qualities of the full spectrum. This phenomena becomes apparent to us all through the millions of droplets of water within the rainbow, as it does through a single prism.

Newton also observed that many birds' plumage or beetles' scales in fact are not coloured. Their surfaces are actually transparent or perforated, giving the ability to disperse and refract the light that falls upon them separating them into their component frequencies of translucent like colours. Birds, animals and insects owe their perceived colours to pigments of their reflective qualities such as haemoglobin, melanin, carotene and chlorophyll, which are some of the elements creating those reflective qualities of nature. Pigments have the ability to absorb certain wavelengths from light and reflect a single wavelength to the eyes, giving us the perception of colour.

Therefore colour doesn't exactly exist until this information reaches the brain. How the brain re-codes or re-constructs it within the mind has not yet been discovered, but neither has the fact that the sub-conscious understands the psychological and physical links to colour.

 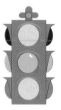 

Colour can be information just like the red stop light which changes to green to signal go. We use this information to identify message sequences, such as if fruit is ripe or not. Doctors in the not so distant past used a form of colour diagnosis observing the colour of a patients tongue, their complexion and eyes, to recognise the colours of specific illness symptoms, blood pressure or dis-ease, as mentioned previously.

In the main mankind has not used the Language of Colour, because humanity has remained under the power of fallen Illuminaries, aligning themselves to duality, black and white. Loosing their conceptual ability to work with other Polychromatic (Colour Coded) vibrational realities.

There is a colour code in every thing!

CHAPTER FOUR

Is Colour a Mere Illusion?

Colour is a mere illusion as it is a specific vibration or frequency split from the full spectrum. More accurately a specific reflection of colour sourced from the full spectrum of light. We can only see reflected images of colour. Objects are not this or that colour, but its surface is capable of reflecting that specific vibration. This information is then sent to the brain which then tells you what you THINK you see.

Colour consciousness is just the beginning of the journey through colour, leading one to colour knowing. Just as we really see colour and start recognising its very important place within us through our different levels of consciousness, we appreciate the influence of the colours of nature, of one's clothes, and of our home or office interiors. This appreciation is recognised through our responses to the colours used to ENGINEER each specific space.

In so many ways we have looked at the CLOTHS of colour, such as the obvious appearance of Red appearing closer and blue receding from us or red appearing warm and blue cool. Learning to visually change the perceived dimensions of a space, we can bring a sense of warmth or coolness to any area be it bedroom, office or factory. To learn and understand the complexities of colour enriches our own perception and enhances our pleasure of all every day occurrences. Glimpses of the hidden messages given by nature in its flowers and awareness of the flower's colour shows to all the world its soul intent, even to where in the physical body it will help to harmonise and heal. We respond to colour and have colour preferences which are the keys to buried emotional structures, which we sometimes call mind locks. It is this personally programmed response to each and every colour and hue which is so clearly linked to our thinking feeling processes.

To learn and understand the complexities of colour enriches our perception and enhances pleasure in our every day lives, from red of the base chakra to violet at the top of the head or crown chakra.

Red induces action, energy, and represents vibrance, but like all energy, each colour just IS. Just how we respond or react to each vibration and frequency, be it in a positive or negative way, *it's our choice*. We respond to colour and have colour preferences, which are the keys to buried emotional structures. Indeed colours are the keys to our MIND LOCKS or as previously stated that which we can term programmed responses. These reactions are gathered from experiences even before birth and added to by our parents, friends, schools and society.

Each of us has a unique perception of this world. Our perceptions colour how we interact with life. We are often brought up on a diet of fear, prejudices and contradictions. We also grow up within certain social, economic and belief systems which are normally very restrictive and this narrows our views and perceptions of our own particular WORLD. This world we experience as real is bought about by so many factors and how we experience this world is hidden deep within. *If we create toxic programs, this leads to toxic thinking, therefore toxic experiences.*

Culture is to humanity as is personality to the individual, something constructed, becoming so ingrained that we confuse it with the essence of life. We become so used to our "own" images of ourselves that we think that our own character traits are indeed the sum total of our individual experience. We learn our own cultural assumptions so well that we consider them to be "Universal Truths". Personality as well as culture are like masks we wear, or roles we play. (pretend to be). Observing that no one seems to take their masks off, we consider them to be their true faces.

Masks are of course a form of pretence, (not necessarily from a conscious level) which we practice from childhood. As we want to be accepted by firstly our parents or parenting substitutes, so subconsciously we pretend to be what we think they want us to be {a programmed response}. A parent or older person can instil their own fears or phobias into an inexperienced child. This adult usually knows NO better, but should.

All human dilemmas are effects generated by previous causes. We may protest on the conscious level that we created this problem, but the effect is always traceable to the cause. Just keep in mind that the subconscious is ever open to suggestion, which our life style constantly dictates. Actions and attitudes create the harmonious or in-harmonious patterns within our lives, that is why it is so important to be a "conscious thinking human being" with an interest in self knowledge.

Become aware of your own self defeating attitudes and actions which undermine your important goals and expectations. When we begin to think about using our full mental and creative powers, with wisdom and a little discernment, a lot of pitfalls are avoided.

Freewill imparts the responsibility of choice when you give yourself permission to step past programs. Using intelligent and ethical choices allows the inherent powers of one's consciousness to create favourable circumstances and conditions within one's present life. We have choice every moment of our lives, it's what we do with these choices that can imprison or set you free. Through increased self-knowledge and understanding, souls can evolve to the next level of expression, moving through the eternal cycles of manifestation towards a higher expression of being.

COLOUR ALPHABET

The Alphabet of Colour is here to show us the way forward to a deeper understanding of "The Lights" higher intelligence by moving us through and beyond the barriers of our consciousness. Colour gives us the signals, messages and codes necessary to direct us through life's great adventure.

The colours of Nature, together with their relationship's with the Sun, Moon, and the Stars, all direct us along our life's path.

Colour and colour combinations are linked intricately to events and circumstances throughout one's life. These events and circumstances can be remembered and recalled accurately through re-accessing colours and their coded messages, which are linked ll to our thinking/feeling processes. Also by linking colour's to events, we can re-read our lives path just like a book. Just by learning the colour alphabet we are allowing ourselves an accurate assessment of colour's coded messages.

 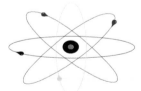 

CHAPTER FIVE

Exploring the Perimeters of the Self Through Colour

We can learn that by quietening the mind and by making positive suggestions to the subconscious, we can change the conditions and circumstances within our external world. We are today once again learning to exercise this power and dominion. In other words we are taking our own power by controlling our thoughts and actions by the use of images projected to the unconscious screen of the mind. This so called unconscious subconscious is really the power behind the throne of consciousness. On the outer level, we rely much on information and direction from our inner levels. Rather like the rudder on a ship, our subconscious steers us through life.

The exploration of inner space has been advanced through meditation and other mind control techniques such as yoga or Mind Dynamics and now the wisdom of colour is being shared. Colour is a focal point for the mind and through understanding colour's ARCHETYPAL FORMS, we can bring the sub-conscious to the conscious. Having the ability to think, conduct, analyse, and create, we are clearly in charge.

What mysteries and ancient truths are there still to be discovered within the innermost depths of our beings? Colour can be a powerful tool capable of guiding a seeker to the answers within themselves. Colour reveals the profound and divine intent to the soul which is prepared to receive this truth. This truth can set you free.

Colour assists mankind in reaching a fuller understanding of sacred knowledge through the subtle expansion of consciousness. As realisation unfolds within the individual soul, the divine plan can be gradually revealed. Remember God shows only so much of His/Her face at a time, as we become more able to accept such revelations.

The keys to future breakthrough's in physics, psychology, psychiatry, and medicine will be given through the cross matching of geometric and colour codes. This will allow the structure of the chromosomes and their light/time participating levels of consciousness to be understood. There is a colour code in everything.

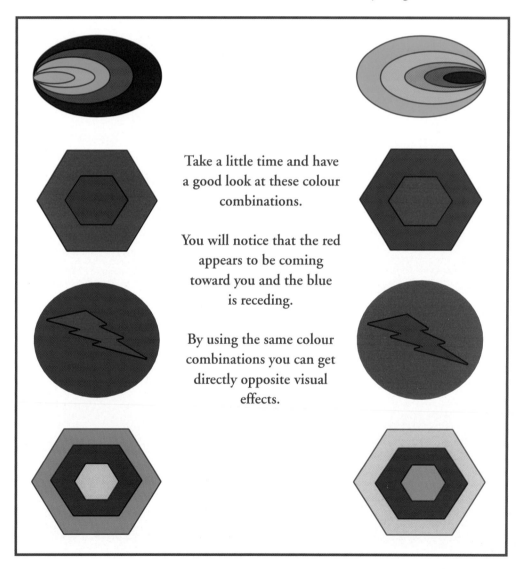

Take a little time and have a good look at these colour combinations.

You will notice that the red appears to be coming toward you and the blue is receding.

By using the same colour combinations you can get directly opposite visual effects.

CHAPTER SIX

It's All in the Mind

"Know thyself," this is phrase that has been echoed through the centuries, not only by great philosophers, psychiatrists and thinkers like Freud and Jung, but also by great masters and teachers such as Christ, Buddha, Krishna etc.

Great importance should be placed on one's state of mind. The levels of negativity are the most critical, as this is where all our problems begin. The negative mind seems to be the inherent nature of our human minds, focusing much of our attention upon it. It is said that we spend 90% of our thinking on emotional responses. By not accepting this present reality regardless of what we have created, we are seemingly never satisfied. Just like a monkey, we are always grabbing and looking for more.

What of the negative mind that creates emotional disappointments which can then enter the physical body's internal and external relationships. It is usually assumed that we will always have difficulties throughout one's lifetime but these are in fact keys or opportunities to personal growth. We should be ready to learn each lesson and move up a grade in the stairway of life, thus creating specific qualities of being. These qualities are rather like beautiful gems which we bring forward in a positive mode helping us to complete our life's purpose. Remember that the quality of your life is brought about by the quality of your thinking. So take care about what you are thinking.

When We Change Our Minds, We Change Our Lives Experiences.

Through the thinking feeling processes we recognise what response is appropriate at any particular time. This internal interaction produces a cocktail of chemical messages which spread through out the body, bringing harmony or dis-harmony, balance or imbalance, ease or dis-ease. If any of these chemical responses is over energised, the body will have to react or even over react.

There are two main responses, put simply positive or negative, love or fear. As we now realise that fear {emotional responses} can be controlled, even understood, no one makes us emotional, angry, or frustrated ... we decide to be. Therefore we can choose, that means you can, decide not to be any of these things. Other people also do things and say things which we decide to get upset about, and that's just it, we decide. It is us in the beginning and it is us in the end, we are in charge. We are indeed only what we think we are.

Using choice to tap into the cosmic code

With every thinking/feeling pattern there is an archetypal pattern within corresponding colour combinations which can be used to accurately and quickly diagnose what archetypal pattern is now in use. More than that, we can look at past and even future potential patterns. Firstly the seeker is required to be instructed in a simple but accurate method of choice or some would say "dowsing", which will be explained in more detail later. In fact a choice can be made for any slot within one's lifetime revealing not just the physical disposition but the creative program behind it. Unicorn 2000/Aura Light Harmony bottles have 80 combination of colour, just awaiting translation. Colour never lies but occasionally mistakes can be made in translation if the translator doesn't follow the given keys in a positive intuitive way.

To create an accurate consultation and to reveal a seeker's life flow and future path, we need to choose bottles that aim for certain slots which can give the information required. We start with a choice covering one's early childhood, this being where our main programs are laid down, followed by ones perceived main obstacles or challenges reoccurring from the past, sometimes not dealt with yet. This is also a time of gaining wonderful qualities of being. The third choice should cover the here and now, a today choice, followed by a choice for the future potential that you are attracting into your life. This process will be dealt with in depth later.

It seems quite clear that our subconscious understands colour, which in itself has very specific vibrational values. Know that when we expend a specific vibration you must then receive a specific response, {result}. What you give you get, which is the definition of KARMA. We must also recognise that we choose that which we need, even to a harmonising vibration in our personal clothing, the colours of food we eat, even to a relationship. Choice if understood and directed, can be a very useful tool within one's lifetime. A choice made with the right hand, links to the left brain which is related to fear programs, logic and systems. It rarely tells one the truth, but will tell you what you THINK you need.

The left hand choice links firmly with the right creative, intuitive side of the brain, before programs, accordingly a much more accurate aspect to choose from and not restricted by negative programs. A choice made with this hand will tell you, what you really need, rather than what you think you need.

CHAPTER SEVEN

Your Imagination is Your Link to...
The Cosmos, God, the Light.

When imagining the basic structure of the universe, one should think about the overall universe as holographic in nature, but in essence a thought form projected by GOD, the creator's choice of expression and Self-experience. This thought creation can be looked upon as a spectrum of consciousness, represented here by what are loosely called The Rays. If there is a point of origin for creation centred within our universe, then this would be the origin of The Rays.

Rays are considered to be a spectrum of consciousness within the mind of the creator, which permeates all creation on our level or planes of existence as they refract through etheric geometric forms. The Rays are an essential factor within our creation and the evolution of that created consciousness. The central point within each galaxy within this universe can be looked upon as a minor duplicate of the central point of the universe ... A RELAY STATION. Many stars are step/down relay points or receiver/generators.

Our sun being is our nearest relay station, bringing the many influences from our second sun SIRIUS, together with our neighbouring astrological frequencies. The sun's basic geometric form collects energy patterns from each planet within our solar system, then modifies and generates to our seven chakras channelling energy patterns through our solar plexus and on to our more subtle levels.

This brings stability of function and awakening of consciousness within each chakra.

For example Chakra 1, planet Earth promotes stability while Pluto stimulates the expression of consciousness.

For each of the five chakra's above the head, there is a stellar influence to promote the expression and consciousness, as well as a ray to stimulate and awaken these energy centres. Crystallising of these energies help to bring about our physical reality which is achieved through geometric forms, basically the 5 platonic solids. These are closely associated with the 5 elements which are the fundamental formative patterns of creation as far as we can perceive it at this point in time.

The Rays don't move in the sense of space/time confines, as they are beyond these elements, but manifest as an essential component of conscious creation, the spectrum of the spiritual consciousness of the universe. The creative and evolutionary forces including The Rays, Geometric Forms, Astrological and element energies are found in a variety of combinations within plants, crystals, etc. which can be transferred to us through essences prepared from these sources, promoting natural healing through, harmony, balance, activity and growth.

Unicorn 2000/Aura Light products are carefully prepared using selective crystal attunement and transfer together with stabilisation and energising patterning as well as essences carrying a vibrational component which consists of a synergistic selection or Harmonic Structure of Rays, Star, Planet, Geometric Form, Gem, Mineral, Shell and of course Flower's, together with other important frequencies such as musical notes.

Their preparation involves a Marcel Vogel specially cut quartz crystal which is used in a specific procedure, which resulted from experiments by Vince Halpin and Dr Marcel Vogel's both in Australia and the U.S.A. at his Psychic Research Laboratories in San Jose, California.

The combinations of essences, essential oils and colours within the external preparations, create a total "Enchantment" of influences, adding an additional visual and olfactory stimulus. This energy trigger's the opening of our consciousness to new insights of being. As these powerful vibrational essences enter our system, they move through our magnetic fields and make contact with the meridians and enter the nerves and blood. From this point of transfer, energy moves into the physical cell level as well as aspects of our other subtle levels, such as the chakras and aura. Steroids, alcohol, caffeine etc., interfere with these pathways and can hamper the effect of any VIBRATIONAL PREPARATION.

SUBTLE BODY ASSOCIATION'S.....
Causal .... Collective consciousness; Cosmic energy Link.
Soul .... Higher Self; Link with the Creator.
Spiritual .... Spiritual aspect of all bodies.
Astral .... Personal History; Past lives & Hereditary filter
Mental .... Mental Activity and clarity.
Emotional Etheric ... Emotional activity & stability; Secure feelings.
Etheric .... Etheric & Physical interface; Life Force medium.

White Light

CHAKRA 11   Chakra 12

CHAKRA 10

CHAKRA 9

The five chakra's above the head are placed on the continuing spiralling matrix connecting to the physical body only through the outer finer etheric bodies.

CHAKRA 8

CHAKRA 7   **Crown**

CHAKRA 6   *Brow*

CHAKRA 5   **Throat**

CHAKRA 4   Heart

CHAKRA 3   Solar Plexus

CHAKRA 2   **Lower Gut**

CHAKRA 1   **Base of spine**

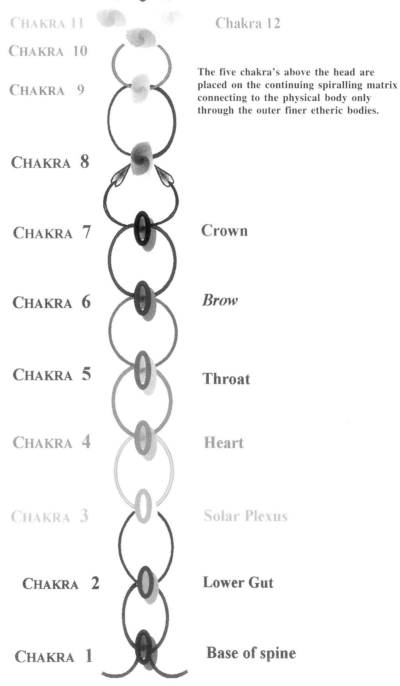

The Rainbow Serpent
The Kundalini Energy flow up the spine crossing at each chakra.

CHAPTER EIGHT

Chakras...What Are They?

Chakra is an ancient Sanskrit word meaning wheel. They are in themselves spinning vortexes of energy. Located within one's etheric body, these energies are able to transmit the light codes containing the processes of life to each chakra, these being a focal point for the life forces which relate to the one's physical, emotional, mental and spiritual levels of being. This is a network for the body, mind and spirit to interact within. This system helps to maintain balance between the endocrine and physiological systems where the physical chakra's are the transformers of Cosmic Energies.

The seven major physical chakras correspond to specific aspects of consciousness and function, whilst having a corresponding relationships to specific glands and organs as well as a specific colour and it's vibrational value. These are the seven colours reflecting the rainbow spectrum. It is said that chakras are but doorways for one's consciousness to receive and distribute cosmic energy to our many levels of being. They feed our body/mind mental/emotional structures, energising each cell (being a unit of life in itself), tissue and organ within the physical body, as well as their related areas in life, such as love, power, emotions, survival, communications and so on.

When all the chakra energies are in harmony, our body, mind and spirit follow, or we should say that when there is harmony of body mind and spirit, it results in harmony within all chakras. One's entire body/mind system is a connecting link to all other levels of universal consciousness. Each and every one of us are interconnected.

We are within a holographic reality being part of all that is, which allows us to open up ourselves into a greater expression of our own potential of unconditional love, thus connecting us to our higher selves and linking us to all of humanity on a higher collective level. Simply put, chakras are energy vortices on the etheric level of being which distribute energy through the nadis or minor energy points (rather like an etheric nervous system) to related areas of the physical body.

The seven major chakras are rooted in or near the spine. The next five important chakras are located above the head within the continuing vortex energy spiralling above. There are also hundreds of minor ones distributed throughout the energy levels of our system whilst the basic twelve chakras are associated with certain aspects of consciousness relating to mental and emotional processes and Spiritual awareness.

It is said that the Meridian System interfaces with the physical systems as well as the Etheric Levels of being. One's Etheric Body energises most aspects of the physical expression and is closely connected with any expression of disease within the physical body.

Chakra associations

● The chakras are energy vortices on a subtle level of being, the major physical ones being rooted to the spine.

● Each chakra is associated with the energetic levels of activity of particular endocrine glands, nerve plexus and organs.

● Each chakra is attuned to specific colour, sound and planetary influence.

● Each chakra reflects the functioning of particular aspects of consciousness related to mental, emotional and spiritual processes.

● If a chakra is referred to as closed, this chakra's activity is minimal or well below normal.

● If a chakra is referred to as open, this chakra is functioning actively.

● If a chakra is referred to as balanced, this chakra has balanced activity neither too active or under active.

- If a chakra is referred to as awakened, the individuals consciousness is attuning to and integrating the special aspects and qualities associated with this chakra.

- One's overall health is strongly influenced by one's chakra activity and inter-chakra alignment and harmony. Chakra functioning varies according to one's mental and emotional state as well as growth. Once a chakra is fully awakened in the deepest sense, one's spiritual aspects associated with each particular centre becomes integrated into one's own consciousness and way of life, assisting spiritual growth.

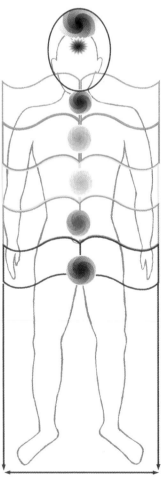

CHAPTER 9

Six Plus One Chakra System

Do we have a seven chakra system,
or what I call a Six plus One Chakra System?

When we consider how our 6 + 1 chakra system correlates to colour and the colour wheel, we see that the three primary colours are used, also the three secondary colour plus just one tertiary colour Indigo which represents chakra 6. A tertiary colour is a combination of a primary and secondary colour, which in the case of Indigo, is primary blue and secondary violet. Indigo relates specifically to the third eye or brow chakra which is said to externalise the pituitary gland and act as a key to the Seventh Chakra, thus allowing that chakra to find its true potential of communicating and revealing our higher levels of being to one's Self.

You can see why they say that this chakra 6 corresponds to the horn of the Unicorn bringing Inspiralisation of energy to the third eye. The horn through the ages has been depicted as Gold, the harmonising colour or after image of Indigo. Therefore we could say this is the Golden Key to unlock the mysteries of the Universe which for so long has been hidden?

Each chakra has a specific planetary vibrational correspondence and each chakra is being fed energy via the Sun passing energy patterns through our solar plexus. The Sun is the transformer station for this planetary to physical energy. Indigo has a correspondence with the planet Jupiter, the only planet in our system without a planetary counter balance. The other planetary to chakra to colour links are paired to a harmonising frequency.

Indigo's correspondence with the metal tin is interesting as the spectral line of bichloride of tin falls exactly on the frequency of Indigo. There is also a correlation between tin and the planet Jupiter.

Indigo is Blue = communicating, combined with Violet our spiritual being. Therefore the third eye or chakra 6 main purpose is not a physical one, but a spiritual one linked to our finer and higher levels of being, which remain unseen.

Colours have very specific qualities of action and interaction, one to the other. ie. Red & Green cancel each others energy creating white. Blue & Orange, and Violet and Yellow create white and have the potential to cancel each other by adding up to the three primary colours created from white. But Indigo is the only chakra colour left alone, remaining without a balancing companion to complete the transformation back to white light. Rather like Jupiter being un-complemented, its character being fixed. The pairs of planets mentioned have gravitational relationships. Jupiter alone is without any VISIBLE counter balance and was called AMON, the master of the skies by the ancients. It is interesting to note that Zeus and Jupiter were one and the same.

Correspondences between, colour the elements and planets.

Red = Fire = Mars. Complementary to Green = Mercury = Mercury.

Blue = Water = Venus. Complementary to Orange = Sulphur = Sun.

Yellow = Air = Moon . Complementary to Violet = Salt = Saturn.

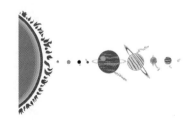

CHAPTER TEN

Chakra Associations
The First Seven Relating to the Physical

Chakra 7. Eastern name: Sahasara, Activating Colour: Violet.
Location: Crown.

- Chakra seven is the highest centre of input for spiritual energies to be used and distributed through the many energy systems of the body. This centre, being more on a higher frequency level has little to do with imbalance or disease states of the physical body. The degree of awakening of this chakra is directly related to its integral relationship of the sixth chakra the Ajna centre. This gives spiritual attunement on a feeling level via the heart chakra. With the awakening of chakra seven, comes a stronger link with cosmic energies, a greater spiritual awareness, and a closer identity and integration with the Oneness and the sense of fulfilment that comes with this. This chakra leads us beyond the physical senses and elements.

Chakra 6. Eastern Name: Ajna. Activating colour: Indigo.
Location: Brow.

- Chakra six is associated with philosophical concepts, innate wisdom, clairvoyance, inspiration and practical accomplishments of lofty aims. It externalises the pituitary gland and is said to be the key to the spirit. When activated, this chakra gives an all round view, far seeing & bringing psychic abilities, inner attunement, spiritual growth and deeper understanding.

Chakra Link Chart

CHAKRA Location	Nerve Plexus	Physiological System	Endocrine System	Related Colour
CROWN	Cerebella Cortex Pineal	C. N. S. Central Control	Pineal	VIOLET
BROW	Hypothalamus Pituitary	Autonomic Nervous System	Pituitary	*INDIGO*
THROAT	Cervical Ganglia Medulla	Respiratory	Thyroid	BLUE
HEART	Heart Plexus	Circulatory	Thymus	GREEN
SOLAR PLEXUS	Solar	Digestive	Adrenals	YELLOW
SACRAL	Sacral	Genitalia	Leydig	ORANGE
BASE	Sacral Coccyx	Reproductive	Gonads	RED

Chakra 5. Eastern Name: Visuddha. Activating colour: Blue.
Location: Base of throat.

● Chakra five is associated essentially with communications of self expression. It is associated with the thyroid gland, which in turn governs the vocal cords, bronchial apparatus, and metabolism. When activated, local energy flow brings a more balanced activity with greater self confidence through self expression and the communications of ideas.

Chakra 4. Eastern Name: Anahata. Activating Colour: Green.
Location: Heart area.

● Chakra four is associated with feelings of love of others, compassion and harmony through well considered judgements. It externalises the Thymus Gland which in turn governs the action of the Heart, blood and circulation.

When activated it can bring a new and understanding of inner peace and harmony with greater compassion and expression of love, including self love. Also brings a better balance and expression of the other chakras, together with greater attunement to and expression of Divine Love.

Chakra.3. Eastern Name: Manipura. Activating Colour: Yellow.
Location: Solar Plexus.

● Chakra Three is associated with the vitalisation of both physical and etheric levels of being and is the seat of nervous disorders. It externalises the pancreas, governs the nervous system and the action of liver, spleen and gall bladder. It also influences the digestive and assimilation systems and energy distribution in general and is associated with will power and its programmed responses based on fear. This is where we can take control of our lives from clearing sensitive issues of personal power.

When this chakra is activated it restores normal chakra activity increasing local and general energy flow, bringing greater mental and emotional control and improving metabolic activity.

Chakra 2. Eastern Name: Svadhistana. Activating Colour: Orange.
Location: Sacral Area.

● Chakra Two is associated with creativity, not only in a procreative sense or reproductive level but also on a relationship level and mental and emotional levels. When activated chakra 2 restores and improves energy flow and circulation to local areas of the lower gut. Helps open one up to greater initiative and creativity, improved relationships with your self and then others. The holder of the keys to far memory.

Chakra 1. Eastern Name: Muladhara. Activating Colour: Red.
Location: Coccyx.

● Chakra One is associated with self survival instincts, fight or flight and basic understanding of this physical dimension. This chakra externalises the Adrenal Gland which is associated with the spinal column.

When activated chakra 1 restores improved energy flow and circulation to the associated areas of the physical body. It helps to initiate Kundalini activity, also helping to release past issues (anger and frustration) in order to move forward. Chakra 1 is associated with life drive and the expansion of your horizons.

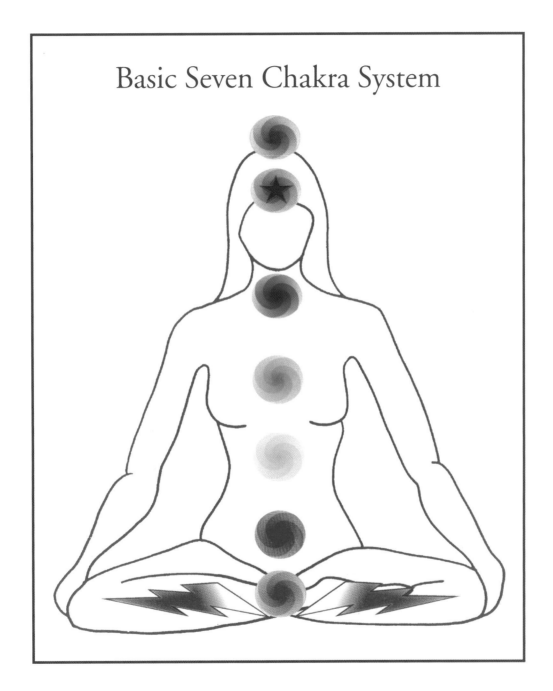

Basic Seven Chakra System

Seven Chakra Basic Associations

Chakra 7. Spiritual energy flow, Cosmic energy Link.

Chakra 6. Insight, Inspiration. "Inner Communications".

Chakra 5. Self expression, Communications.

Chakra 4. Balance, Centredness, Compassion, Heart, Love.

Chakra 3. Emotions, EGO, Will.

Chakra 2. Interrelationships, Deep Emotions.

Chakra 1. Survival Instincts, Grounding, Sexuality.

There is a dual planetary influence on each of the first seven chakras to promote stability of function as well as the awakening of consciousness within these chakras.

Chakra One, for instance has a planetary link to Earth which promotes stability, also another to Pluto which stimulates the awakening of this chakra's level of consciousness. For each of the five chakras above the head, there is a stellar influence (Not a planetary one) to promote and expand their consciousness and to bring a Ray energy to stimulate the awakening of each of these chakras.

Chakra complementary colours....

Each chakra has a vibrational link to a specific colour which in turn has a complementary colour. (As seen within an artists wheel) The three primary colours have a secondary colour as their complements, other than chakra 6, Indigo, which is a tertiary colour and has a tertiary colour as complement.

Red   comp. Green = blue + yellow   includes the three primary colours.
Blue   comp. Orange = red + yellow   includes the three primary colours.
Yellow comp. Violet = red + blue   includes the three primary colours.
Indigo comp. Gold = yellow + orange. Gold is a tertiary colour.
INDIGO = (Violet + Blue) secondary + primary = Tertiary Colour.

Every other physical chakra colour is either a primary or secondary colour. Indigo seems to be quite separate in nature, linking only to the third eye or brow chakra. When we look at the unicorn horn we can see that traditionally it has been shown as golden and firmly based on the brow chakra (Indigo), drawing inspiration and inspiralization of energy allowing us to find the very best of our being.

COLOUR WHEEL

Showing Harmonising – Complementary colours

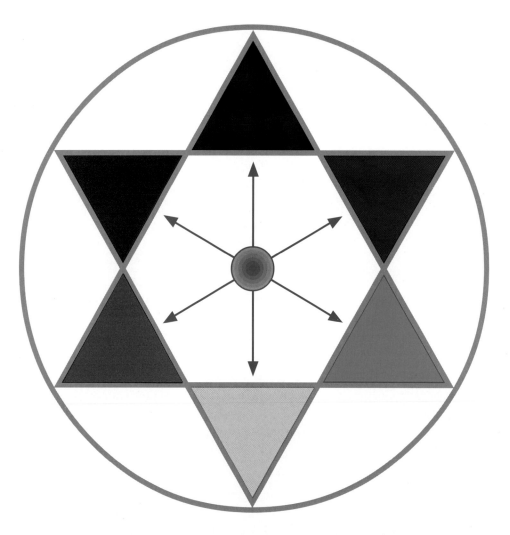

Each pair of complementary colours contain the three primary colours.

The third eye....the control centre of the soul

There is some very interesting research being done on the pituitary, pineal and thyroid glands and their relationships' to one's spiritual/psychic and imaginative senses. The pineal is believed to be sensitive to other forms of radiation, such as electro magnetic fields, which play an important role in dowsing. The third eye is reported to be linked to both pineal and pituitary glands and in esoteric terms it governs the lower brain and nervous system, ear's/nose and left eye, linking to ones lower self the subconscious. The pineal is said to be the glandular expression of the crown chakra, being the focal point of the spiritual will and seat of the soul. When the third eye opens, the soul then has a perfectly direct avenue into other dimensions.

We have within the brain a mechanism to create our own inner light, often perceived by enlightened and spiritually advanced beings. The pineal has been compared to an alchemical retort vessel which can release its spiritual essence into mankind if and when the dross has been burnt from our personality and in so doing, transforming us into one of the bearers of light, so necessary for this New Age.

The Cabalist aligns Binah with qualities of Divine Understanding and Hockman with the qualities of Divine Wisdom, to the SIXTH CHAKRA.

Binah represents also the womb of the divine mother, able to receive the seed for conception. Hockman has also the quality of The Beginning.

The unity of these two energies is linked to the principle of Form follows Thought. We indeed command energy to become matter.

This gives the Sixth chakra the qualities of unique insight which seeks only the truth which lies between one's illusions by using the inner direct path of power and insight of the impersonal mind.

The Unicorn has been linked through time to the Virgin/Empress who symbolises all containers and channels of nature. The gold of the unicorn horn is as magical today as in ancient times if one understands that gold comes from the illusional relationship of yellow and orange.

The brain commands the body whilst the mind commands our other energy bodies which relate to thought and perception. The brain being a physical instrument is capable of transforming thought into action. The mind is associated with perception and consciousness. It has the ability to detach or more correctly assume an inner posture of neutrality, separating the external influences from the subjective perceptions, thus finding the truth and hidden meanings, with clarity of Self. Becoming conscious of being means living consciously within the present, working through constant change. It is the illusion of the physical, that holds us prisoner, stopping us enjoying this constant change of life and being and finding the higher truths which lie behind all change.

Our attitudes are deeply involved with our health in supporting or destroying the body, by directly affecting one's immune system, thereby handicapping our healing processes through fear, hate, bitterness and resentment.

Remember the power behind positive thinking is expectancy...What you have imagined and now expect.

Other...chakra associations....

The higher five chakras are situated above the head & seated into the continuing spiral of the Kundalini energy flow as shown in the Rainbow Serpent diagram.

● **Chakra.8. Not recorded in ancient times.**
  Activating colour .... Magenta
  The eighth chakra is associated with the awakening to our cosmic links beyond earth. The opening of this chakra helps one harness these supportive energies and helps promote a deeper self identity as well as opening one to channelling. It creates a greater willingness to serve mankind in an unselfish way.

● **Chakra.9. Not recorded in ancient times.**
Activating colour .... Pink
The ninth chakra is associated with lifestream purpose and function within reality. With the opening and awakening of this chakra comes a greater clarity with regards to one's life purpose as well as a better assessment of one's progress. This chakra helps with increased perception regarding astral level experiences and the dissolving of personal barriers to true expression of self identity, as well as assisting with a greater attunement with Universal Divine Love.

● **Chakra.10. Not recorded in ancient times.**
Activating colour .... Turquoise
The tenth chakra is associated with the harmonising of one's emotions together with one's spiritual needs and reaching a greater accord with the forces of the Universe. By opening and awakening, this chakra helps harmonise motives and actions in accord with one's spiritual goals, linking deeply with one's intuitive faculties. It also helps promote heart/mind balance to better achieve the soul's purpose of clear expression and helps lift states of depression or negativity. Through deeper harmony one can better co-operate with the forces of nature.

● **Chakra.11. Not recorded in ancient times.**
Activating colour .... Gold
The eleventh chakra is associated with the active "Yang" principle and dynamic forces of nature. The opening and awakening of this chakra brings knowledge that one has the ability to achieve one's life purpose as well as a sense of duty to achieve that purpose.

It also helps move one out of lethargic states and promotes a greater awareness of "GOD" as the active element in all things, together with a sense of this presence within one's own being {The GOD within} and this develops greater fatherly love.

● **Chakra.12. Not recorded in ancient times.**
  Activating Colour .... Silver
  The twelfth chakra is associated with the passive intuitive "Yin" principle
  within creation and one's innermost link to the creator, our Divine Essence.
  With the opening of this chakra, one becomes aware of their divine purpose.
  Also with the realisation that all things will be achieved according to the divine
  plan, there comes an increased inner feeling of freedom of the spirit.

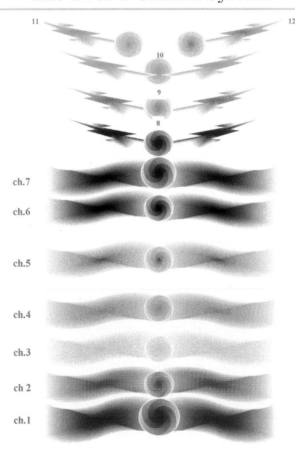

The Twelve Chakra System

CHAPTER ELEVEN

Basic Structures of the Cosmic Code

Colour appears within our everyday lives in so many subtle forms, it seems that colour's familiarity prevents us from recognising many layers of consciousness. It is only through study that we can start to look past its surface structure and realise to what extent colour is working so efficiently upon and within ourselves and our environment. Colour gives animated and inanimate forms specific qualities which then transform them into what we perceive as people, landscapes or even seasons.

The colour coding of our races, our seasons and our countryside, create a kaleidoscope of visual qualities to be married to form. My quest over the past thirty odd years has been to go a lot deeper into our understanding of colour's hidden qualities and secret codes, and this today is recognised as the science of colour.

This science acknowledges and establishes colour's relationships with all other forms and notes established similarities and any interconnectedness together with any Laws which are interrelated, or any philosophies that connect them.

Colour as we know, can help us to regain inner harmony as it connects our intellect with our emotions, releasing the soul to show its true expression. Each and every being is a Cosmos within themselves, expressing a unity of a harmonious whole. Mankind needs to communicate with each other as well as the environment around us, as it is through this coded exchange that we are motivated through life. We are exchanging and transmitting the many frequencies being received on our multiple levels of consciousness, not just physical, mental and emotional but on our many subtle levels of being and life energy. Colour interacts with us through a mirroring of our energies. This reflection occurs on so many levels, opening us up to new processes of thought and feeling.

Colour carries an enormous potency in terms of growth and change, owing to its existence within natural laws, through which it finds its expression within the physical and tangible forms. Colour helps us to recognise the true nature of what we call creation. This creative force follows the Cosmic Laws of Chaos and Order, of positive and negative, of Love or Fear. Each colour has a very specific vibrational quality that can be used or perceived as expressing these qualities of chaos or order. Chaos leans to the dissolution and clearing of the past, bringing about the possibilities of the creation of new expressions of life and allowing for expansion into new ordered forms. Order then builds and keeps life within its proven structure. Both poles together assure a living system which is flexible and able to expand and go forward. (Death & Re-Birth)

Colour's effect upon our consciousness is multi-dimensional, having an energising effect upon all levels. In the main we are not aware of how dependent we are on colour within our daily lives. Scientific studies have shown that we could not survive without the frequencies of colour. We absorb these frequencies through our food, skin, eyes and more.

Individual colours stimulate specific organs and glands within our body and without this stimulation our systems will break down easily. There are so many ways to use or apply colour that can help bring back an energetic harmonic structure to the body, mind and spirit.

As mentioned earlier, each colour and hence each chakra is closely related to one of the 5 platonic solids and 7 crystal structures on a basic atomic level. Each of the geometric forms throughout the realms of primary creation itself has it's own corresponding numerological and axis code which describes its very own unique configuration and light activity principles. It is important to understand that these geometric crystallisation patterns are the basis of the cosmic code of light activity principles, the seed format of colour. These lattice like templates (levels of consciousness) allow the higher frequencies of light to flow, creating the diversification of the visible and non-visible spectrum of frequencies.

We could say that they are the basis of a great Universal Alphabet of limitless combinations that form the causal matrix creating relationships with light on

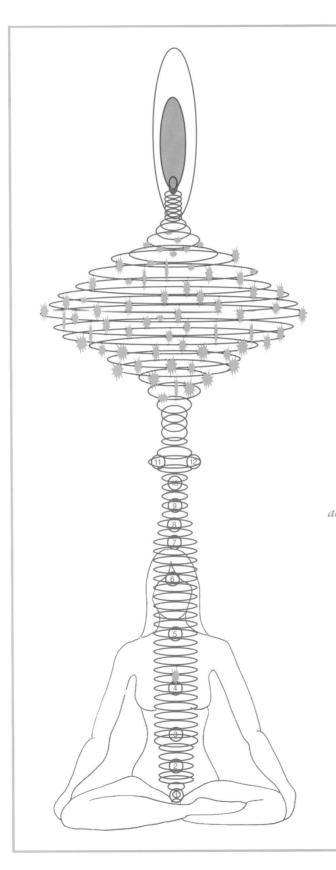

I Believe

You *are a wonderful
multi-faceted Being of Light.
Most beautiful to behold*
You *being
Just one facet of that
Being, which is you.
That facet resides behind the
breast bone.
Each time we come forward in*
Truth *and* **Unafraid**
*we build a new light molecule
within our physical .
Living this your body can
accept another facet of your higher
being.
You would then be called*
Enlightened

multidimensional levels. These light codings formulate and interact on any dimensional or level of being. This great geometric and numerological alphabet is the governing principle of light creation. Colour is the visible key to this code offering us a way to understand it's cosmic links.

Let there be light................

Light is a form of radiant energy that has no mass and no electrical charge, but can create protons and electrons, the building blocks of the Atom and thus the Universe.

According to the Quantum theory, light is transmitted in "pieces" of action called Photons, the basis of this physical world. Photons are units of light which seem to be motivated by a specific purpose. It is said that photons form a ray of light that will always take the quickest path through the atmosphere to reach its destination. Light seemingly has intelligence which has been called, "The principle of the least action." revealing that there is a definite purpose behind the causes of this material world. The theory of relativity predicts that time does not exist within the world of photons which travel through space without any loss of energy. Light cannot really be seen, but simply makes seeing possible. Light holding colour within it, is part of that intelligent force whose existence is proven mainly by the phenomena that it creates. We, in this time, have a concept of light that categorises it as a force which is pure energy, timeless and spaceless. Light is all pervading of the whole Universe, with a limitless infinity of purpose and action. Light is Life.

Just observing colour's can alter our moods, our energy levels, therefore our physical body.

CHAPTER TWELVE

Complementary Colours, Harmonising Colours

Complementary colours are those that sit opposite each other within the colour wheel, and they are also (importantly) the after image of each other. If you stared at a red spot on a light back ground for a few minutes and then looked away to a white or light coloured surface, you would still have an image of a green spot, which takes a few seconds before dispersing. An example that comes to mind, was a problem that some workers in a pill packing department had. In the 1960's they still counted pills by hand as they were put into bottles. Unfortunately the continual focus on red was giving the workers headaches, simply because they saw green dots before there eyes as they looked around. The simple solution was to paint the walls green, hence no more green spots and no more headaches.

How we see colour.............

Atoms make up all objects. This is an invisible energy with electrons orbiting around a nuclei. As light strikes a surface, only certain rays are reflected back while others are absorbed. A complete absorption of all rays and frequencies result in the appearance of Black. It is when all frequencies are reflected back we then see a White. Whatever frequency is reflected, say 7500 angstroms, in this case then we would see Red and all other frequencies would have been absorbed. We only see red when there is a light source otherwise all would appear black. Our bodies are a mass of vibrating molecules, which in turn are a mass of vibrating nuclei of protons and the like which are tied to the cosmos with invisible strings or force fields, electrical and magnetic energies, and colour frequencies.

Disease and illness are energy blocks, disturbances or imbalances within our finer energy systems reflected in cellular imbalance. There are many contributing factors and one of these is that the wrong messages are being passed to the body, through previous wrong connections to the thinking/feeling programs.

It is said that colour is to the soul as air is to the physical. It is therefore life giving. Colour liberates us from the strangle hold of the physical, through the understanding of the soul. Colour allows us to not only find and follow our dreams but to also recognise and weed out inappropriate hidden programs.

The power of colour illuminates every single aspect of our lives and has strong psychological effects upon us which in turn influences our feelings, disposition, attitudes and condition of health.

We often choose colours symbolic of our intentions and desires, our likes and dislikes which add up to a fairly accurate personality profile. By choosing clothes, make up, goods or home furnishing's we often reflect our current moods, as well as deeply hidden programs and problems.

Dr Max Luscher devised a psychological colour test to assess one's mental, emotional and physical health and this has been used in the past by the medical profession with some success to identify some causes of illness. This system uses a set of eight single coloured cards, as follows:

0. Grey
1. Blue with a violet tinge
2. Green with a turquoise tinge
3. Red with a slight orange tinge
4. Yellow
5. Violet with a purple tinge
6. Brown
7. Black.

The enquirer is required to shuffle cards and then lay out, colour side up in the order of preference. This is repeated a few times, taking note of the colours chosen, which is then followed by an equation. This was found to be a reliable, accurate system by those who have made a thorough study as it was in a 1948 study.

Today building on the great work done by Dr Max Luscher and his contemporaries, we have been able to push the boundaries forward once more, so that now we are able to present The Aura Light/Unicorn 2000 Colour Diagnostic System which I believe to be the most accurate in the world.

The boundaries still have a long way to go but I believe we are in good hands with new pioneers coming forward now and in the future to show us all the way by using psycho dynamic associations and application of colour combinations as ways of understanding the many subconscious levels of being.

Relationships....

Relationships are one of the most fundamental aspects of being, embracing the case of duality, which in turn leads us to the next step which we call the trinity. This encompasses a third aspect or property. If there is two, the relationship of these two becomes its third property. This has left me wondering if there is such a thing as duality?

We can explore this a little further with the following information from the great Seal of Solomon.

Male ...		Female ...
King ...		Queen ...
Sun ...		Moon ...
Father ...		Mother ...
Will...		Imagination ...
Yang...		Yin ...
Right Hand ...		Left Hand ...
Conscious ...		**Sub-conscious ...**

The law......the heart.

The great Seal of Solomon is a figure of symbolic as well as functional significance, representing the decent of spirit into matter and the ascension of matter into spirit, continually taking place within the cycle of eternity. In many cultures this is represented by the snake (The Rainbow Serpent) which is also a symbol of wisdom.

The star has six points as we can see, but the seventh point exists as the centre point. We must remember that without a centre point a star could not exist. To have knowledge of this sign, means to know or realise the nature of "GOD" and the Laws of that eternal nature, together with the process of evolution and involution. All are working through the microcosm of nature.

The enlightened one sees the invisible, seeing the primordial Rays of Light.

White Light being the most potent energy of the Grand Architect of the Universe can be perceived as a circular spiral being able to manifest the Trinity. Holding then within it the balance of Yin and Yang energies spiralling throughout an etheric medium, or multiple levels of energy and being, expressing mankind's state of dynamic equilibrium. The seal also represents the "Marriage" of the Kundalini and primary forces. These are shown by two interacting triangles, one descending, the other ascending and coming to rest in harmony at the heart. This union creates a current which bears the light to the body. The super imposition of the Active and the Passive Ternaries produce a SIX POINTED STAR which is the principle of multiplicity, divine order and destiny.

Colour in the hands of a skilled practitioner is believed to be able to work with universal energies to amplify and to harmonise body energy, (emotions and memories) helping to bring them to the surface and into one's consciousness where they can be dealt with properly. Using the right energy patterns which link to deeply hidden memories these can then be recalled, examined and then released.

In many cases these hidden memories or programs turn out to be the root cause of current illnesses or dis-ease. We all create the world we perceive and all perceive according to "Impressions" set in the past.

Unicorn 2000/Aura Light Harmony Diagnostic System is an invaluable tool to reveal attitudes, needs and one's psychological make up, spiritual leanings, philosophical views, educational propensity, as well as the ability to love and express one's emotions. Also our relationship's with one's parents becomes apparent, as does compatibility within existing relationships, together with our latent talents and creativity.

Colour can also reveal both physical and Karmic patterns, linking these to the attitudes now held, from which we translate the outer world to the inner. Colours are as it were, messengers of the spirit, an ancient yet modern messenger ready to speak to seekers and healers everywhere. So we can see colours are the windows through which we can transcend our EGO. That EGO which is so closely linked with our thinking/ feeling processes. Through these ancient roots we can link firmly to other levels of consciousness and even to our Spiritual Origins and Essence of Being, which in the main we have forgotten.

Surely the Great Seal of Solomon even in this day and age has a very special message to pass on to us. If we have the eyes to see, the relationships of opposites are the purpose of manifestation, realisation then leads to illumination, which is created through relationships.

Our multi-levels of human functioning, reflect the old adage "As above – So below."

We are today recognising the primary role of one's life forces through the use of colour, which is at the cutting edge of vibrational medicine with its ability to interact with the body's unique energy systems and the capacity to re-organise ones physical and cellular framework. By organising and nourishing these subtle energy systems, we help them to co-operate with the physical body. It seems that conventional medicine has been misled by the notion that you cure illness by treating the symptoms rather than the cause.

Unicorn 2000/Aura Light's colour diagnostic system allows for the cause to become visible and indeed accessible and to be treated on an individual energetic level and also to transform the human consciousness and the spirit that animates the physical framework which we call the body.

One's consciousness is registered on many levels of being, down to the cellular levels and beyond. If you can change sufficient quantity of this consciousness on a cellular level, this change then registers on the outer conscious levels, through the deeper interrelationships of mind and body and spirit working with the natural laws that they function within.

Working with the cosmic patterns of nature and natural laws at all levels creates energetic structures of healing and re-creation. There is a quiet revolution on its way.

Unicorn 2000/Aura Light colour harmonics is a modern development of a very ancient healing art, conceived through meditation and channelled information, nurtured and developed over many years through the co-operation of Vince Halpin and myself. This has culminated in a very unique range of colour and vibrational healing systems, encompassing so many facets and ways of linking colour.

Australian wild flower essences, herbs, essential oils, and crystal energies. These powerful packages of heavenly combinations, each having its own integrity, are put together to not only enhance each others vibrations, but to create specific harmonic structure tools for the use of mankind.

We must recognise that we are uniting a number of different therapies all together within one medium. Colour therapy, aroma therapy, herb and gem therapies are not just adding to each other but are multiplying and magnifying the power within each tool.

Unicorn 2000/Aura Light is a self empowering therapy for the complete being, bringing healing through harmony by using colour's energised wavelengths as the chosen vehicle. Every tone and shade of colour is the perfect messenger for its precious cargo of healing wavelengths.

By establishing harmony with the use of these combinations we can restore ease to our system, thus creating a balance of the being, well being so to speak through complementing the bodies natural ability to restore balance and ease to itself. A healthy body is dependent on the condition of the aura and free flow of energies through the chakra centres where blockages can result in disease, illness and imbalance. With the manifestation of disease alone (being its symptoms) the cause still remains to surface again at another time.

Those colour frequencies of the aura when weakened can be revitalised and replenished by applying Unicorn 2000/Aura Light formulas.

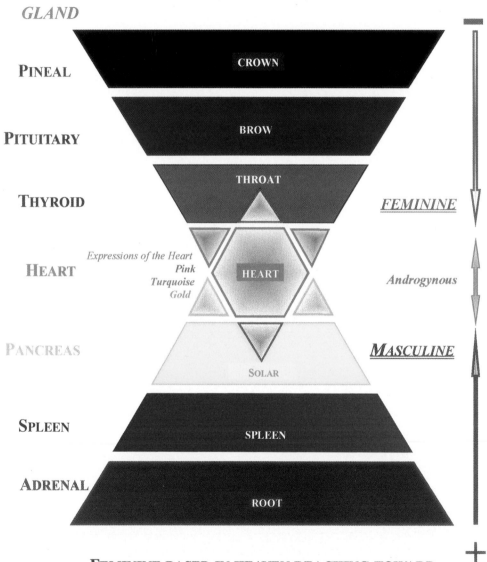

Undivided Light

FEMININE BASED IN HEAVEN REACHING TOWARD THE EARTH.
*****

CHAPTER THIRTEEN

Meridians. What are They?

There are twelve major meridians which represent specific frequencies of life force flows which supply the driving force for the organs of the body. These meridians can and are effected by our thought form patterns. Other meridians are much more involved with the integration of life force flows throughout the complete system. Central energy channels for both the front and back of the body flow vertically so as to energise and stabilise the whole system.

Subtle bodies... what are they?

The subtle bodies are highly refined individual energy fields set around the physical body and are associated with certain aspects of being. For example when our thoughts are registered within our Mental Body, our emotions within our Emotional Body are then registered within our Astral Body. Colour and vibrational remedies can help cleanse and align the subtle bodies to promote stability, balance and growth with the levels of personality and consciousness.

Planetary influences

SUN .... Basic life force, Vitality, Circulatory system,
MOON .... Emotions, Body fluids, Female organs functioning,
MERCURY .... Comprehension, co-ordination, Bronchial system, Cantral
                     nervous-system
VENUS .... Circulation, Female organs, Tissue relaxation.
MARS .... Muscles, vitality, Blood formation, Male organs, Motor nerves.

JUPITER .... Arteries, breathing, digestion, Liver, Pancreas.
SATURN .... Skeletal system, Skin, Solidification, Self discipline.
URANUS .... Aura, etheric body, spinal cord & brain membranes.

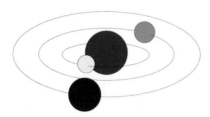

As we have seen with these few examples of various energy patterns and the part that they can play within a client's healing process, we must recognise that to heal, one needs to clear any disturbed patterns and restore normal energy flow. Together with the removal of any causative thought patterns we must then develop specific aspect's of consciousness that may be lacking. Aura Light/Unicorn 2000 products contain all of the above energy pattern associations and much more within its various products giving an in depth co-operation of energy patterns from various sources creating a Harmonic structure of healing energy patterns.

CHAPTER FOURTEEN

Personality Colouring

What are your true colours?

Colour in itself has its own personality, just as we have. If we look at what are the colours that our lives and personality correspond with, this may tell us where in the rainbow we are.

RED....Physical....Base of the spine.
The red personality when positive is: active, pioneering, spontaneous, practical, and sexual.

Reds can choose energetic and high risk professions such as Racing Car Driver, Construction Worker, Dancer, Boxer, footballer etc.

They like to do things NOW, therefore live in the present.

They need physical contact, intensive activity, and sensory gratification. They have a need to sense beyond the physical, To plan before action, and to become perceptive.

When in negative expression they can show impulsiveness, anger, violence and over-reaction.

Summary of Personality:
These are pioneering people sometimes extroverts, and they like to do and dare. Therefore sometimes a little impulsive and passionate within work and also within relationships.

ORANGE...Social, spleen, lower gut.

The orange personality when positive is: Expansive, Warm, Optimistic, Competitive and Altruistic.

It can choose professions like, Social Workers, Receptionists, Stewards, Diplomats, Personnel Officer.

They like to do things now but for the future.

They have a need for social contact and acceptance within a group or family, together with respect and a good reputation. They have a need to belong to the family of mankind, through love and service, making deep contacts with others.

When in negative expression they can be seen to be, selfish, superficial, anti-social, emotional, over stressed, manipulative and proud.

Summary of personality:

These are some of life's best organisers, quite often with a gift for languages and quite often they "like" their food. They are also always on the go and looking for peace and quiet. They are great feelers, linking strongly to any injustice, their own or others. This group tend to be extroverts and very sociable and may be larger than life. Need to be more content within there family structures.

YELLOW....Intellect Left Brain... Solar Plexus.

The yellow personality when positive are: Logical, Analytical, Self Aware, Methodical, Precise, Good Planners and Organisers.

They often choose professions like. Teachers, Researchers, Computer Programmers, Technical Writers, Mathematicians.

They like to link the past to the present, then to the future.

They have a need to discover the heart in order to end separation and to merge with the ALL, thus having conflict free situation within relationships. They also need to shine intellectually and to understand, and overcome their doubts and fears.

When in negative expression they can become, Contradictory, Judgmental, Separative, Unfeeling and Fearful.

Summary of Personality:
They can be very intellectual types and make good students and researchers. Good at logic and money matters. Left brain activity. When in positive flow, can manifest Joy and Happiness, but always looking for wisdom and truth. At times, yellows find it difficult to assimilate food and learning. They have a need to separate their intellect from their fears.

GREEN....Security...Heart.
This green personality when positive are: nurturing and generous, open hearted and compassionate as well as expansive.

They could choose professions like, Counsellors, Gardeners, Florists, Healers or Veterinarians. They like to link to the past, present and future, seeking security and approval.

They have a need to: Love without attachments and to overcome possessiveness and insecurity. To learn to save...to love and be loved. To be free.

When in negative expressions: There is a tendency to self doubt, insecurity, jealous, to be miserly and mistrustful of life.

Summary of personality:
These are people coming from the heart and they are wanting to harmonise with others, linking very strongly with nature. They tend to take on others burdens and problems. Greens also like to keep moving and would dislike any sort of restriction although they do create them within their own minds. Greens look for freedom from what has been, and continue to look for their right place and space. By learning to open their hearts, the mind and body can follow.

BLUE....Conceptual...Throat.

This personality when positive are: Idealistic, loyal, committed, patient, nurturing, nostalgic, peaceful.

They could choose professions like: Teaching, Historian, Missionary, Teaching of Meditation or yoga, or complementary practitioner.

They like to remember and live in the past and always searching for their inner truths. They could have a need to attain inner peace, to find mental security and to live an ideal life and also to conquer self righteousness.

When in negative expression: They tend to be too self satisfied, dogmatic and resistant to change, rigid, ultra conservative, and slow to respond.

Summary of personality:

They could have a strong sense of conservative nature, Quite often the nurturer of the world and blues can be perfectionists. They are mostly cautious of deed and word whilst having a great need to communicate. Visualise them as the writer, the singer, even the artist. Can be very critical of others as well as themselves, but have a need to follow their own ideals not those of others. They would have a strong link to the mother as a child.

INDIGO....Intuition...Brow.

This personality when positive is: Sensitive, far-seeing, visionary, inspired, and psychic.

Could choose a profession like: Advisor, Inventor, Actor, Poet, Artist or Diviner. They would like to live in the future, and discover the secrets of the universe.

They could have a need to: have a conflict free relationship, feel at one with the universe, manifest dreams into one's physical life and to be grounded .

When in negative expression: They can be introverted, spaced out and not living in the NOW, ever forgetful and always late.

Summary of personality:
This would link to a psychic or intuitive person able to link into the truth, allowing them to be very skilful in their work place. They are working to bring those wonderful dreams into reality, through having an all round view.

VIOLET....Intuition...Crown.
This personality when positive can be: Very creative, charming, possessing of a sense of wonder, have mystical instincts and the power of transformation whilst maintaining clear thinking.

Could choose a profession such as: Artist, musician, designer, architect or in fact anything creative.
There can be a need to live in the past, present & future transformation through thinking.
They could have a need to bring order out of chaos, freeing the Self from the ego.
Their motto: Transform the Self by the power of thought.

When in negative expression: Being the day dreamer, having a bad self image, becoming too introspective, being overwhelmed, egocentric, being quick to take offence and so feel misunderstood.

Summary of personality:
Very intuitive but also a very sensitive person having a need to explore these characteristics through art, music and spirituality. These qualities were gained through an early inner journey, sometimes a retreat within. They find happiness there rather than within this physical life. A creative person able to use their well developed imagination to manifest and create. There are those who would rather be off with the fairies, rather than to face and interact with life. They must use their imagination to produce positive results within life and for their self image and stop giving in to fantasies.

CHAPTER FIFTEEN

Now is the Time of Seeding the New Age The Age of Light.

In Christian terms it is called *The Shift of The Ages*.

The Mayan's called it, *When time Stops Still*.

In real terms it's the *Age of Re – New – All*.

In New Age terms it is called *The Quantum Leap Forward*.

Colours as mentioned, have very specific vibrational qualities which are measured in wavelength meters, as are Gamma Rays, X Rays, Ultra Violet Rays.

Colour comes into our visual range or visible light between 10.6nm and 10.7 nm. nanometers, (Nano = one thousand millionth of a unit) and is followed by Infra Red, Microwave's and then Radar, Radio, TV. etc.

This is called the electromagnetic spectrum. "The Spectrum of Light" {and Life}. Colour occupies a very narrow band within a very much larger spectrum of Electromagnetic radiation.

As humans, we are continually bathed in unseen radiations, quite varied and diverse from radio and TV to solar energies including Ultra Violet Radiation etc., together with other man made frequencies produced by fluorescent light, overhead high voltage wires for example and the list goes on.

We have learnt to recognise that we interact on many levels with many frequencies, but must find if there is indeed a rightful place for them within our own personal life.

Now we must learn that many positive subtle energies play an important part within our daily lives and we now need to recognise their promise for this coming new age. At the end of the nineteenth century a Scottish Physicist, James C Maxwell, identified that all of the above are in fact belonging to the same range of frequencies, although appearing to be so very different whilst still having characteristics in common. This range of Electro magnetism behave as waves of radiation from their specific sources, and travel through space in straight lines at a speed of about 186,00 m.p sec. This spectrum is measured in metres, but some radio waves measure some hundreds of metres long.

The wavelength of visible light is very much shorter in fact .0000005 shorter. Therefore light is measured in "nanometers" = 10 to the power of 9. Visible light which contains the full colour spectrum falls within 380nm and 760nm.Generally light itself is approximately 500nm. The wavelength is measured from the crest to trough or top to bottom of one cycle of vibration between two crests or troughs, the frequency is the number of waves per second. (see diagram) As light is composed of a number of waves with different wavelengths and frequencies or rates of vibration together with its amplitude, each component wave on striking a prism is reflected at a different angle. Red being the longest wavelength but lowest frequency has the least refraction and appears at the top of a rainbow, but violet being the shortest wavelength yet having the highest frequency has a bigger refraction and appears as the lowest colour within a rainbow.

NANOS, is the Greek word for nine.
10^9m. (1 000 000 000)

10 – 16.	Wavelength Meters.
10 – 15.	
10 – 14.	Gamma Rays.
10 – 13.	
10 – 12.	
10 – 11.	X. Rays.
10 – 10.	
10 – 9.	
10 – 8.	Ultra Violet Light.
10 – 7.	

VISIBLE LIGHT

10 – 6.	
10 – 5.	Infrared Light.
10 – 4.	
10 – 3.	Microwave.
10 – 2.	Radar.
10 – 1.	F.M. Radio.

T.V.

10 – 00.	Short Wave.
10 – $_2$.	

A.M. Radio's Electro Magnetic Radiation's behave as wave's radiating in all directions (Multi-dimensional) from their sources, travelling space generally in a straight line, at a speed of 186,000 m per sec.

The Rainbow

Rain Drop

Direction of Light

A RAINBOW is bought about by sunlight reflecting through a mist of rain droplets ranging from as small as . 01 of an inch to as large as 3/8th.of an inch.

We perceive the Rainbow's primary bow at approx. 41 deg. Violet appearing at 40 deg. Green at 41 deg. Red at 42 deg.

40 to 43

The secondary bow is perceived at approximately 53 deg.

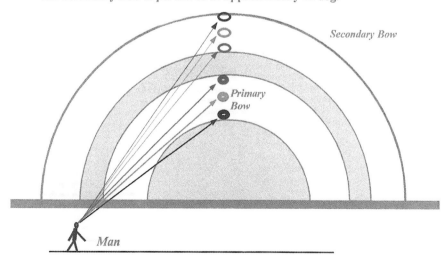

Secondary Bow

Primary Bow

Man

When passing light through a prism its second surface refracts the emerging light rays again dispersing them more widely. The light rays emerging are "Not Coloured" and only become visible when they strike a surface, thereby giving a reflection we then perceive as colour. Passing a single colour through a prism doesn't break down into any other colours, only white light forms the complete spectrum.

Sir Isaac Newton did a lot of early scientific research within our modern historical times, where he looked at the properties of light and colour, proving many of the theories we accept today. Newton also concluded that all "SPECTRA" are formed by the action of light striking transparent objects such as glass, drops of water, etc., which behave like miniature prisms. He also noted that each colour had a different reflective quality.

It is interesting to note that a projection of Red, Blue, and Green of equal intensity onto a white board will give a white light effect where all three colours overlap.

There are some other combinations that will give the same effect. Surprisingly, it is not easy to get the three primary light projections to fuse into White Light.

Primary and secondary bow Rainbow

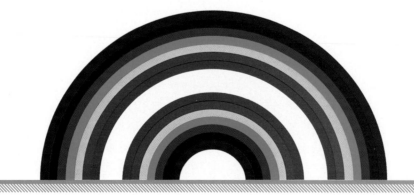

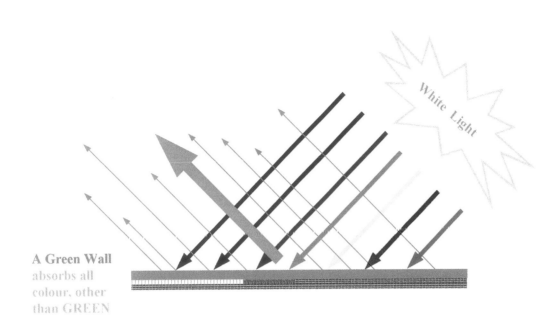

A Green Wall
absorbs all
colour, other
than GREEN

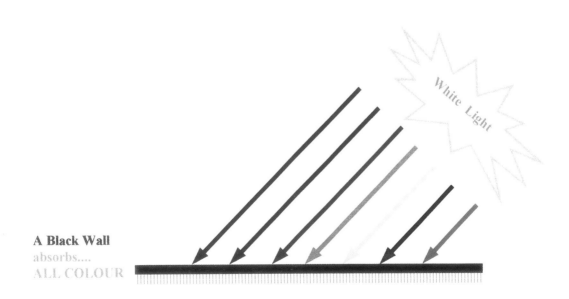

A Black Wall
absorbs....
ALL COLOUR

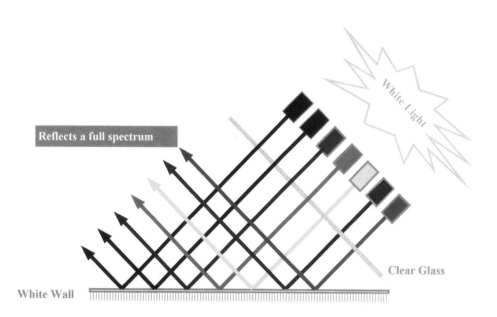

Reflects a full spectrum

White Light

Clear Glass

White Wall

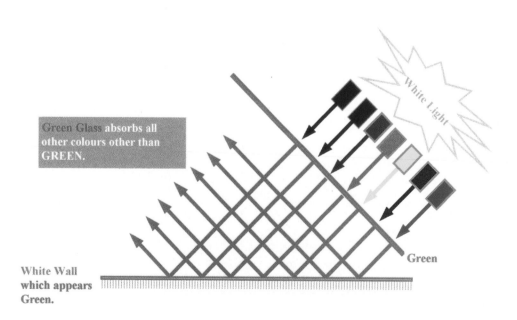

Green Glass absorbs all other colours other than GREEN.

White Light

Green

White Wall which appears Green.

CHAPTER SIXTEEN

Through Choice "We Choose What We Need"

Basically we choose what we need, therefore a choice for the past represents a need from the past, a choice for the future represents the potential or gift for the future, a choice for today represent a little of each.

We are using colour as a means of triggering the subconscious to reveal the hidden depths. It is also a system that anyone can use, and is equally precise and accurate no matter what your background of social, economic or belief system.

You can become your own counsellor, revealing exactly what you want and "therefore need" to know. Truly it is a self revelation, giving insights and prompting one to look into the depth of the soul, allowing us to take our lives in to a new dimension.

Using colour is the key to new and deeper levels of awareness, which allows for a much better understanding of the meanings of life itself, this added self knowledge helps one become the actor rather than the re-actor to life.

Become your own 'oracle'.

An oracle is not only as many people would think, a psychic or medium, but someone who can show you the way. Just by using our inbuilt dowsing ability which is revealed by our left hand choice, you can choose using this natural sense which is a simple way of bringing the unconscious, subconscious to the conscious. By following this process, it will enable you to differentiate between what you think you need, rather than what you know you need. The difference is shown through the left or right hand choices. We need to make sure that your different levels of consciousness are fully aware of the choice subject or slot that you are making the choice for ... your past, present or future for example.

The clearer and more defined we make the target slot, which happens through clear, precise details given and held within the mind, the closer to your truth you will be. This setting up works in conjunction with the eye, meaning that the eye is the mind switch, with the ability to switch from right to left brain according to which hand the choice is being made from. Using the left hand and removing the right from sight {say behind your back} present the left hand in good view, ready to make choices? Now you mind has been switched and your need to concentrate on the target choice. Being that this choice is based on a four bottle target choice, let us start with a choice representing you as a child within a parenting situation....

This time slot is when we pick up so many of our long held programs, not always with our natural parents, hence parenting situation. The need at this time for a young soul is to accumulate certain qualities to complete its life purpose. This we achieve through perceived problems and hardships to overcome, creating those beautiful gem like qualities required for our soul's progress through perception in the now. The second choice needs to encompass obstacles or challenges which seem to repeat themselves mainly through not being addressed properly, so they come back awaiting completion. This reveals our progress and development.

The third choice covers the here and now, what's happening within our physical, also revealing the creative programs that have created any physical imbalances, (symptoms) together with gained qualities for your progress.

The last target choice is in many ways very fluid, showing our future potential. It could also be said to be the future you are attracting towards yourself. Once we change in the here and now our future potential changes. Change you mind and change your life's experiences and expectations. One's potential comes from our "earned" qualities, therefore only positive qualities apply.

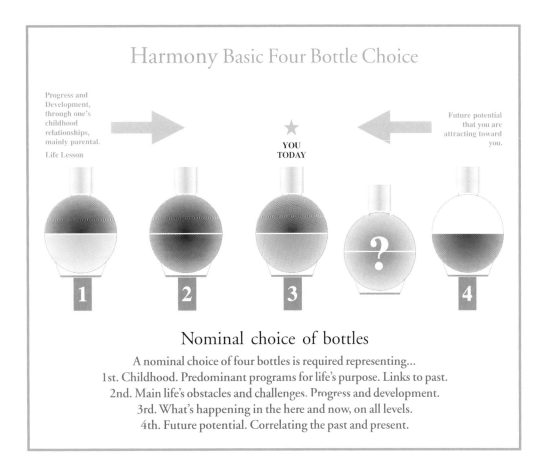

Harmony Basic Four Bottle Choice

Progress and
Development,
through one's
childhood
relationships,
mainly parental.

Life Lesson

YOU
TODAY

Future potential
that you are
attracting toward
you.

1 2 3 ? 4

Nominal choice of bottles

A nominal choice of four bottles is required representing...
1st. Childhood. Predominant programs for life's purpose. Links to past.
2nd. Main life's obstacles and challenges. Progress and development.
3rd. What's happening in the here and now, on all levels.
4th. Future potential. Correlating the past and present.

Missing colours..................

It should be noticed which colours are missing from the completed selection, which relate to circumstances a little hard to look at, or require looking at, allowing your future potential to come into existence without impedance.

Notably the no.5. bottle carrying the yellow and red responses, is simply a release mechanism for old emotional programs and wounds, which are in themselves blocks for future spiritual progress.

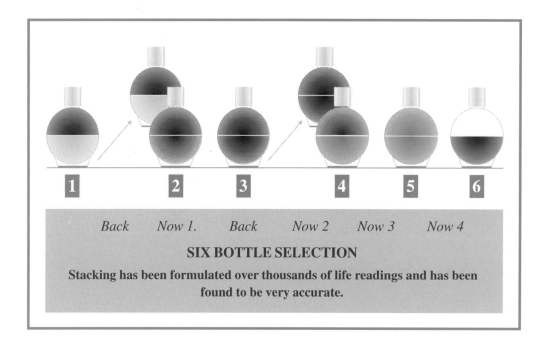

	Back	Now 1.	Back	Now 2	Now 3	Now 4
	1	2	3	4	5	6

SIX BOTTLE SELECTION

Stacking has been formulated over thousands of life readings and has been found to be very accurate.

Mis-match.............

Life is a cycle and has links between our beginnings and our end. Therefore the choice of bottles within our selection, is itself representative of one's life cycle or life flow. To see this we need to see the integrity of links between the first and last bottles....... The link being within the colours themselves. If this link is not achieved, it can represent resistance through subconscious blocks, and also when the seeker is prepared to look at "more". At this point stacking comes into play, but generally in more than 95% cases, when set up correctly there is a link within the four bottle choice structure.

If the match is not evident, this is a time to use your intuition and either ask the seeker to relax for a few minutes and then get re-focused and make a further choice. It has been interesting to note that the majority of seekers making extended choices have been teachers themselves of some kind, but after re-selection has been made their choice has been absolutely accurate. More about colour links later.

Stacking or grouping for multiple selections..................

When a selection exceeds the nominated four bottles, a grouping is necessary. The following has been formulated after thousands of life flow consultations, for accurate reading.

Diagram of stacking....

I would recommend that all extended selections be limited to under eight bottles, or what ever number you feel confident with. The re-selection will always be fewer bottles. If there are eight bottles creating two distinct rows, we can see that very often this translates into seeing two levels of that one person. The front row usually represents what the seeker wants others to "see" of them, the back row showing more of the inner person and the energies being promoted behind their lives at that time. So we can say front row could be the facade of what they want others to believe, but the truth hides behind.

Colour links within choices..............

As each colour has very specific qualities they also tell specific stories, many time a paler version of a colour tells a very similar one, but not always. I would accept the following as good links.

All Deep Magenta, Magenta, Violet, Pale Violet, comes under the **VIOLET** story.

All Dark to pale Blues, and Indigo, come under the **BLUE** story.

All Dark and Light Greens, come under the GREEN story.

All Dark and Light Yellow's, Gold's to Orange, under the   story.

Red, under the **RED** story.

Pale Pink, Pink {pale red} also Pale Magenta, under the PINK story.

Turquoise is a special case and has to be left with your intuition, whether you feel the links to blue or green and maybe other bottles covering relationships. Comes under TURQUOISE story.

Clear, gives a match with all colour as it contains all colour.....comes under the CLEAR story.

Position of colours within bottles ....

Each bottle is dual toned or simply has two colours, a top and a bottom section of expression. The top level of each bottle represents our conscious level of being, and being on the top can appear to be quite dominant, as in say a red. But when we look at all the colours there is quite a range of frequency interchange. Green for instance is giving approval for what is laying within the depth of a seeker, to come forward into the conscious levels, whereas clear represents a need to make good decisions about what lies below and the will power to make these discussions. Blue over is an easy one at first sight, just communions of that which lies below, where as pale blue links to communications within one's higher levels, through meditation etc.

The lower or bottom section represents the subconscious, which is in so many ways the power behind the throne of consciousness. We need the constant input from our many levels, which in the physical we may not be conscious of. Things change when we start co-operating and accessing these levels through the many techniques such as Yoga, and Meditation which are available to all these days. If a colour is based in the lower section of the bottle say once again Red. . . .We know red is anger, frustration even procrastination, Red is really energy, and energy in the sub-conscious in internalisation of that energy.

Where as in the top half of a bottle, it is externalising that energy, rather like an extrovert. Remember that colour just IS. It is what we do with each colour frequency and how we express it, which is important. Green in the lower portion of a bottle gives the impression of someone looking for a new place and space for that inner being, maybe feeling a need for freedom. But more than that, Green is the heart and it is being protected within the inner self. With this knowledge of single colours and their archetypal values as well as their physical relationships it should give the READER sufficient information to understand these simple inner meanings.

CHAPTER SEVENTEEN

An Al-Chemical Formula

Imagination, the wife and constant companion.

The water or the moon can take the shape of the container into which it is poured They are not discriminating and can wander off in any direction, so must be kept in view.

The Moon {QUEEN} can only receive the element of light from the Sun {KING} and become a marvellous, adorable woman. So the Divine Laws can intervene so as to "Accomplish" on the material levels, through THOUGHT, the Divine Child.

Once again we see the basis of our New Colour understanding.

SUPER CONSCIOUS....The Child .... VIOLET .... Steam.

SUBCONSCIOUS .... The Mother... BLUE .... Water.

CONSCIOUS .... The Father .... RED .... Fire.

Within alchemy, spirit has a relationship to steam which is closely connected with water from whence it came. Water is said to be cool and flows, falling on fire creates the steam, which carries with it vivid impressions of the "distillation" of the spirit from water. This al-chemical transformation produces a clearing of the eyes which enables the philosopher to see hidden secrets. Water also holds within it the state of innocence being the water of paradise that makes man whole and immortal. It is the coming together of the masculine/fire and the feminine/water that creates the Steam or Vapours of spirit. Water also links one to the waters of the great subconscious. The divine waters of alchemy contains the healing and renewal properties of this symbolic water.

Al-chemical texts tells us how the highest {Violet} descends to the lowest {Red/Blue} and the lowest ascends to the highest. The mid most {Heart, Green} draws near to the lowest and also the highest, so that they are made one with it. This is how the blessed water came down to awaken the dead, {The blue feminine/subconscious being the force behind the throne of consciousness being red/masculine.} and how the elixir of life comes and awakens them, rousing them out of their sleep. {The great unconscious masses}

Water, it is said by Jung, is not only the hiding place but also the dwelling of the great treasure. He also said that this three fold process holds the Body/conscious, Soul/subconscious, as well as the Spirit/super conscious together. This process transforms substances together in order to produce an end result of revealing the Opus, the Treasure which is hard to hold.

This process as shown by colour, unlocks complexities that even great commentators such as Jung found difficult to appreciate.

The living fire of the holy ghost as philosophers and alchemists simply called FIRE, is the physical facade of our true beings and has been expressed as the direct intervention of God. Being alive = Adam. (The first manifestation of God on earth through mankind.) Living fire, Red, Conscious, Man who mingles himself with the living water, Blue, subconscious, Woman. Thus liberating the spirit, is Violet, super conscious, Child.

Aqua permanens was the "Spiritus Mercurialis" within water and form. Thus water is equated with fire, although these terms were indeed used indiscriminately and are not the same as fire is active. The spiritual fire as a form of "Spiritus Mercurielis" is spiritual, cool, and closer to the subconscious. Both are necessary to the al-chemical processes, since this is concerned with the union of these opposites.

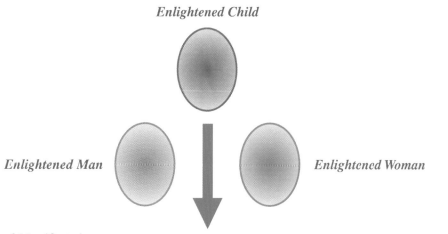

Before Manifestation

Enlightened Child

Enlightened Man   *Enlightened Woman*

Physical Manifestation

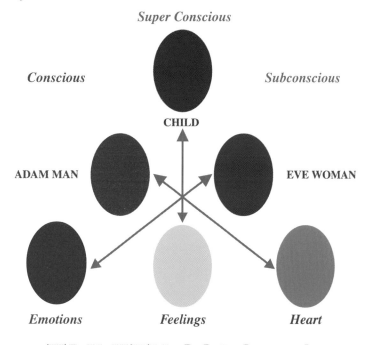

Super Conscious

Conscious   *Subconscious*

CHILD

ADAM MAN   EVE WOMAN

Emotions   *Feelings*   *Heart*

TRINITY COLOURS

Colour is a subjective experience

CHAPTER EIGHTEEN

Our Undercover Colours

Our physical bodies are composed of the following:

9.1%	Hydrogen.	(H2)	**Red**
13.4%	Carbon.	(C)	Yellow
2.5%	Nitrogen	(N)	Green
72.0%	Oxygen.	(O)	**Blue**

Water H2O = Red/Blue. Masculine/Feminine.

By looking at our base components, we can become more aware of the inner levels of colour co-operation.

We can now look at the colour wheel as seen by artists, interior decorators and the like. It is important to start at the beginning with a straight forward look at single colours. The universe has given us the RAINBOW as a prototype of colour sequences running from red at the top through to violet at the bottom, recognising that there are three primary colours, red, blue, and yellow, each having a lighter form, such as pale blue, pale red = pink The secondary colours have mixtures of each pair of primaries, such as Blue and yellow = green, yellow and red = orange, and red and blue = violet. Tertiary colours which have combinations of these secondary colours and so on, have the possibility to produce many thousands of hues.

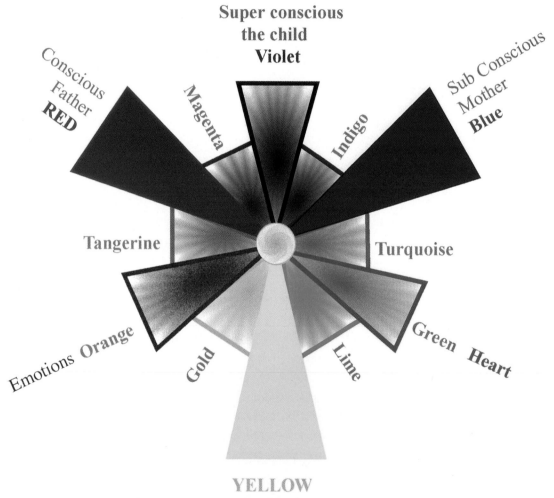

Super conscious
the child
Violet

Conscious
Father
RED

Magenta

Indigo

Sub Conscious
Mother
Blue

Tangerine

Turquoise

Emotions Orange

Gold

Lime

Green Heart

YELLOW
Feelings

Colour wheel

The majority of colour wheels used by artists have a very similar base as shown below.

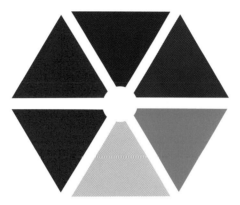

Complementary colours are those that sit opposite each other within the colour wheel. As you can see red/green, blue/orange, yellow/violet. You might also recognise them as after images, which are produced by staring at say a red spot for a few minutes and then looking away to a white surface to have an image still impressed on the retina. In the case of a red spot there's a green after image, and so on. We can see from these colours that they correspond with the rainbow, with red being situated at the top. But also they correspond to the ancient chakra system, where red takes its place at the bottom, we could say like a reflection of the rainbow. Let us look at the specific values and character of individual colours together with some of their chakra linkages.

RED.. Base, Root, or 1st. Chakra. Yang. Masculine. Warm. Right Hand. Conscious level. Adam. The father. Sound – Lang. Musical note C.

Red is energy, procreation, zest for life, dangers, construction and destruction, being alive, sexuality. It produces restlessness, anger, might and aggression and the will to win, sometimes at all costs. Stimulation, impulsiveness, the blood and circulation, living intensely, the pioneer, extending the horizons of the individual, aphrodisiac, the initiator, the extrovert, survival. .... Red represents all of this..

RED IS SAID TO BE GOOD FOR blood and circulation, building red corpuscles, helping to stop cramps, anaemia, sexual desires. It is an aphrodisiac, extends energy, eases dullness, helps if you are introverted and lethargic, cold, sleepy, arthritic, lacking courage Red also is a blood cleanser and helps to warm the body and stimulate the arteries, varicose veins, reproductive organs and eases back aches at base of spine.
RED HAS LINKS TO. China, Russia, The East, Mother Earth, Ground energies, The red planet Mars = God of War, The red flag = Revolution, The red heart = Respectful passion, The red cross = Sacrifice to aid others, Light red to Aries, Dark red to Scorpio, The cube.

RED links to GEMS and CRYSTALS........ Ruby, Garnet, Red Jasper, Bloodstone, Spinal Ruby, Rhodenite, Magnetite, and surprisingly Smoky Quartz.

The focal point of red light is behind the retina, literally advancing objects and making them appear closer. Red is the nearest wavelength to Infra Red, producing the sensation of warmth. Red is a fast moving colour which catches the eye and quickens the heart, which in it self is a response to dangers by releasing adrenaline into the bloodstream and thus warming the body.

ORANGE.... Lower Gut, 2nd. Chakra, Male, Positive, Yang, Sound – Vang, Musical note D.

Orange is about feeling and sensations, good naturedness and flamboyance, giving one back their self esteem, worth and importance, emotional force, emotion and expression and, pleasurable experiences.

Orange releases from bondage to others and slave to duty and obligations, business matters and contracts and encourages emotional expression whilst removing repression.

It is related to being sociable, ambitious, enthusiastic and leads to a concern for others. It helps also in cases of identity crisis through promoting Self assurance.

Orange is said to be good for....
Bad dreams and bed wetting, lifting self worth and respect, digestion, wind, breaking up congestion and colds, shock and stress, inducing spending, self confidence, auric healing and etheric gapping, balancing attitudes and also in relationships.

Independence, self assurance, improved appetite, relief from allergies, having the wisdom to control the emotions, emotions before and after operations, menopausal disturbances, change of life, far memory shock absorber.

Orange links to ....
Himalayas, Africa, India, Gemini, Leo, Lower Intestines, Kidneys, Lower Gut.

Orange links to GEMS AND CRYSTALS...
Carnelian, Tiger Eye, Orange Sapphire, Amber, Topaz, Fire Opal. Orange is said to link to the mind expressing itself outward and expanding. The individual mind blending with the universe, and the ever expanding Manas, becoming Buddha.

YELLOW.. ..Solar PLEXUS, CHAKRA 3. Positive, Masculine, Yang, Sound – Rang, Note E.

Yellow is mentally adventurous, searching for self knowledge and strong convictions. It is the re-energiser of the mind, promoter of mental activity, ingestion and assimilation, study and thought. Yellow is associated with those who can be stubborn and opinionated, have a good business head and are the protectors of innate wisdom. It relates to higher emotions like joy and happiness, emotional sensitivity, reactivity and reaction.

Yellow is said to be good for.............
Self confidence, studying, liver, gall bladder, nervous system, depression, stomach tension, Ingestion and assimilation of food, skin complaints, flatulence and indigestion, fear, bed wetting, nightmares, self control.

Yellow has links to.............
India, Egypt, Sun civilisations, liver, left brain, logic, gall bladder, stomach, nervous system, mental power, money, Judas Iscariot, Aphrodite.

Yellow links to GEMS AND CRYSTALS......
Citrine, Yellow Fluorite, Yellow Agate.

GREEN .. .. Heart, chakra 4, Yin & Yang, Androgynous, Male & Female, Positive & Negative. Sound – Yang, Musical note F sharp, Communicator Blue + Yellow Wisdom.

Green helps prevent stagnation and represents a new place and space, affections of the heart, freedom, adaptability, harmony and brings good judgements, balance and understanding, maturity and self control, love for humanity, generosity, nature, regeneration, karma or opportunities for new beginnings, breathing space, compassion and co-operation, understanding. caring, stability, giving, growth, willingness and a positive expression of the inner self.

Green is said to be good for ....Heart and chest area, Healing the broken heart, going forward, lungs, new space, new beginnings, unselfish action, justice of the heart, restlessness, self control, acceptance, healing after loss, thymus the gland of youth, flu, blood pressure and it influences the immune and endocrine systems. Green is associated with self assertiveness.

Green links to ....The Star of David, Karma, matters of the heart, The Wheel of Fortune, Libra, Freedom, Europe. chlorophyll. nature, the green man, nitrogen.

Green links to GEMS and CRYSTALS ....Chrysophrase, Emerald, Adventurine, Jasper, Green Jade, Peridot, Serpentine.

Green's ambivalent hue focuses almost exactly on the retina.

BLUE .. .. Chakra 5, Throat, Negative, Cool, Yin, Feminine, Sound Hang, Musical note G, Miriam mother of all mothers.

Blue is nurturing, communicating, peace, faith, idealism, sincerity, expression of thoughts, languages and images, the mother, cool and calm, a natural antiseptic, stability, gentleness and meditation.

Blue is said to be good for...Throat problems, bites and itching, Sleep, eyes, nose and throat, a natural disinfectant, over heating or inflammation and it encourages the production of white cells, soothes and calms the mind, eases palpitations, insomnia, promotes cooling. Blue helps with blood pressure and thyroid problems.

Blue links to...Virgo, The pure maiden that serves others, Chesed, banks, chastity, diligence and dutifulness, The Astral body, Woman, Eve, Pale blue equates to the enlightened woman, Isis, Ishtar, Mary, sub-conscious, Moon.

Blue's links to gems and crystals ...Sapphire, Sodalite, Moonstone, lace agate. The sapphire is said to tie a tight love knot.

It is interesting to note that the most worn "uniform" in the world today is the blue jean, which seems to represent the uniform of life. Seeing that we don't want to appear to be a new recruit but a seasoned campaigner we seem to look for jeans with that worn in look. We are, it seems, quite prepared to pay more for faded jeans and even designer jeans with holes in – proof of a seasoned campaigner in the battle of life.

INDIGO.. .. CHAKRA 6, Feminine, Yin, Cool, 3rd eye, Brow, Sound: Ang, Musical note A.

Indigo is about an all sided view, lofty aims, comforting, pacifying and calming, pure spiritual thoughts, devotion to an ideal, psychic matters, the eye of the soul, contact with the higher self, spiritual communications, a higher level of intellect, insight, imagination and self realisation.

Indigo is said to be good for...Inner communications, neurosis, insanity, deafness, the eyes, inspiration, clear seeing, devotion, insomnia, soothes the nerves and the lymphatic system, melancholy, helps purify the blood stream, helps the spleen.

Indigo links to .....clairvoyance, Self identification, enchantment, right brain, introversion, the key to the spirit and flesh united, the ethers, vibrations beyond this physical world and is where energies gather.

Indigo's links to Gems and Crystals ...Lapis Lazuli, Fluorite, Amethyst.

INDIGO is said to give practical accomplishments of lofty aims.

VIOLET. CHAKRA 7, Crown, Feminine, Yin, Cool, Sound OM, Musical note B.

Violet is creative, service, inspiration, creative thinking, mental strength, inspired leadership, evolution of the soul, religion, spirituality, the gateway to attainment, aspiration, humanitarian, devotion, creative thinking.

Violet is said to be good for...soothing of tension, strengthening the nervous system, stimulating the creative brain, the healer, the poet, the musician, the painter, clear thinking, insomnia, headaches, migraine, eye strain, the overwhelmed, self attainment, purification, mysticism and spiritual things.

VIOLET LINKS TO ...... incense and invocation, the sacred flame of transformation, Saint Germain, taking one toward the source (The Creator), ceremonial magic, service to the universe, super-conscious (Child), The ultimate communication to mans central beam of light – Our being. Self attainment. Yesod. pineal gland and the Lotus.

VIOLET links to Gems and Crystals.....Selinite, Amethyst, Clear Quartz, Diamond.

The expression of some VIOLET hues....Rich Purple – Power.
Royal Purple – Arrogance.
Bluish Purple, Devotion to a Noble Ideal.
Clear Violet – Idealism.
Greyish Violet – Superstition.
Mauve – Inspiration.
Lavender – Intuitive Spiritual Contact.

WHITE... Contains all colours ... Moon ... Individual Spirit ... Cosmic Urge ... The Ray of Creation ... Etheric Body ... Chakra 12.

White links to Spirit, Moon, Pearl, Platinum, All Days and All Months, The No.11. White is said to be good for ...Lactation in mothers, a general Pick me Up, strengthening will power, making good decisions and showing the way.

White links to Gems and Crystals ....Pearl, Diamond, Feminine Clear Quartz, Herkimer Diamond, Zircon. White is said to be Yes while black is No. White is all revealing where black is all concealing.

MAGENTA.... CHAKRA 8. Associated with our cosmic links beyond earth.

Magenta links to The receptive will of the source, The primal force working through the physical promoting a deeper self identity, elevation and purification of desires, the recipience of cosmic energies and stepping outside of our universe. Pale Magenta links to Universal Love.

BLACK... absorbs all colour and is not a colour within itself. Links to Negation and Renunciation, the absolute boundary beyond which life ceases, surrender and a hiding place. Black states... What about me ... I need special attention. Black also means not finding the happiness within society and wanting to withdraw from it, hiding one's light {Potential} under a bushel and considers that existing circumstances are disagreeable and over demanding. Secrets.

PINK ... CHAKRA 9. UNIVERSAL LOVE, which is unconditioned and unconditional.

Pink has the more refined and enlightened qualities of Red like love, romance, affection without passion, the enlightened male. Pink signifies sharing and caring, loyalty and compassion, idealised father image and looking for a loving partnership, Being in the Pink is saying that everything is rosy. The Christ Consciousness, the highest ideals within mankind have pink association.

Pink is good for....balancing the hormone system, healing as the old woman who can heal with just a wink of her eye. When we stress the heart it pulls the hormone cycles out of balance. Therefore pink is always associated with a hidden green.

Pink links to Gems and Crystals......Rose Quartz. Kunzite, Rhodochrosite.

It needs to be repeated that PINK is masculine, not feminine. It is red with 15 parts white, therefore enlightened male. Why then do we put pink on a girl baby and blue on a boy baby...could it be to balance their energies, helping them not to be too masculine or feminine?

Pink links to...Venus, Diana, The Heart, The Star of David, Unity and Harmony between Man and God. Pink, being an expression of the heart always has a second hidden colour which is Green of the Heart.

TURQUOISE.. ..CHAKRA 10, THE WATERS OF THE SUBCONSCIOUS, AKASHIC RECORDS.

Turquoise is ...Intuition, Communications of the heart, Relationships. It is also for communications of inner and outer space, elasticity of the mind, sensitivity, originality and refinement.

Turquoise is good for ....
Asthma, bronchitis, heartache, intuition, throat & chest complaints, difficulties in expressing one's self and neutralising attitudes of self blame.

Turquoise links to gems and crystals............Chinese Fluorite, Moldavite, Celestite, Kyanite, Turquoise.

Turquoise links to................
The waters of the sub-conscious, The Akashic Records, Space, Self awareness and the deep still pool of reflection. Still waters run deep.

Listen to the stirring of the Soul in response to the voice of the higher self echoing a self revealed plan for a new way of thinking, a new life urge.

CHAPTER NINETEEN

Crystals Plus

A new Crystal Age is being created manifesting in so many ways, right now. Today's high tech electronic industry would not be possible without the use of crystal oscillators which are used in so many specialised timing devices as well as controlling the frequencies of radio and other electronic communication devices. Crystals have had an important part to play in the development of computers based on the silica chip (Quartz Crystal). The sophisticated influences of crystals are an innate part of an advancing civilisation. They are truly messengers of the world. Slowly our conscious minds are becoming more aware of information in the past only known to our sub-conscious levels, but now manifesting as a great desire to know and work with crystals. It does well to remember that like us, crystals have multi levels of energy and being. In fact I believe we have a very close relationship with that being within each crystal, closer than most people would like to consider thinking about.

Let us then work together with crystals as co-workers of the Light, experiencing the crystal's many levels of being. We can listen and accept their help in transmuting us to a higher level of understanding and therefore expression. As we experience the crystal, the crystal experiences us and through this relationship is always giving new expression to the physical. One of the main characteristics of a crystal is that it has a constant and true crystalline vibration. Every colour and hue reflected from a crystal has a constant wavelength which when it interacts with water can be passed on as frequency properties which held by the water's electro-magnetic memory. This creates a vehicle to deliver these healing frequencies to others as Gem Elixirs.

When adding other harmonising frequencies from other sources such as herbs, flower, even shell essences and essential oils, we create a powerful harmonic structure. Just add colour then the Magic begins!

Anoint the Director Crystal with a Unicorn 2000/Aura Light
essence and project to waiting grid. Ask for energy
patterns to be transferred.

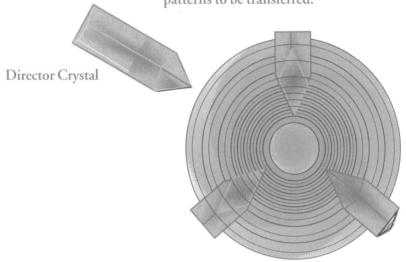

Director Crystal

Simple Triple Crystal Grid Layout

To create a simple crystal grid, place three finger size clear quartz points in.
Make mind contact with these crystals and ask them to create a grid and project it around
the person you wish to project the energy to.

You will now require another finger size or larger quartz crystal as "Director Crystal" this
crystal is anointed with any essence, such as Love & Light, Release, Comfort etc.

This energy pattern is then transferred to the grid and onward to the recipient, which
interacts on very subtle levels of being, making a new level of energy available for the
recipient to use.

We recommend that all projected energy systems should only be used with the recipients
consent or offered for their highest good. It is to be noted that giving Healing or taking
any imbalance or dis-ease from anyone without their consent has a Karmic Dept attached
to it. Therefore this Karmic responsibility goes with the removal of any Karmic learning
process. We have to be very careful that any recipient does not require their illness, or
disease for learning purposes. We all need the ability to respond to life, so that we can
become responsible for our own life.

As the past, present and future are orchestrated by one's life experiences, helping one to attune to the multi levels of the ALL to bring forward an understanding that the ALL is related to our very own multi vibrational energy levels. Once understood, we can use this revelation in many magical ways, allowing insight into gem, herb, flower, stellar essences, platonic solid forms, phonics/music, numerology and especially colour, being in so many ways the visual essence of ALL. Together these energies can and do create a most potent form of vibrational healing.

There is once again a special focus emerging throughout this past decade, being spearheaded by science as well as private individuals and therapists.

Personalities such as Katrina Raphael, Magda Palmer, and scientists including the late Marcel Vogel, and Dr. Frank Alper are helping to bring in a "New Renaissance of Cosmic Healing and Soul Therapies" joining with the many New Age educators.

Numerology and colour   1. 2. 3. 4. 5. 6. 7. 8. 9.

There is a numerical colour spectrum of universal intelligence being reflected through the crystalline matrix of the microcosmic to the macrocosmic levels of cosmic energy. It is transported by light through the many multi-dimensional planes which have been accurately indexed by the divine. This geometric numerical code relates to the colour alphabet and constitutes a font of endless levels of intelligence that has been developed through the selective alignment of our own crystalline matrix base.

This code links to spectrums of limitless intercommunications from the divine order of light. Colour carries with it the abstract intelligence of ordered qualities of numerical and geometric principles which transcend this physical world.

Colour follows exact laws of inter-dimensional physics, which are based upon the quantum harmonic theory that energy exists on quantum levels at harmonious and interrelated domains which we call levels or dimension of manifestation. Colour prompts the process and principles of form through a great variety of key functions, of code matrices to blue prints of the highest levels, releasing data to become us.

Numbers and letters have been associated since their magical origins, from the Phoenician and Jewish worlds and later from the Greek and Roman Empires. It is said that the great Philosophers and Alchemist's of the past considered it impossible to become truly adept without using letters and numbers.

Pythagoras was both a scholar and Mystic who believed that all things resonate to numbers revealing their relationship's one to another. He also discovered their mystical significance by relating numbers from 1 to 9 with universal principles together with their patterns and geometric ratios and by linking music and harmony to the science of numbers based upon Cabalistic principles ... more on this later. Numbers, he said, were the Law of the Universe (later we will show that numbers are the primary alphabet of the universe) and further he said that everything within this universe is subject to predictable progressive cycles, as are the numbers 1 to 9.

Numbers it is said, present qualities, but figures are only used to measure things. A number is a symbol used to convey an idea or an abstraction. Many scientists agree that all possible knowledge is already within the mind or that the mind having access to it, in some abstract form.

Within our minds there lies an abstract world where there is no space or time, therefore the past, present and future blend into eternity. Within this abstract world knowledge is absolute and the study of the abstract comes with the working of mathematics and the communications of the archetypal relationships it presents. Man uses language to communicate thoughts and ideas, one to another in so many forms. The Hebrew language which was used to write the original text of the bible, was originally just numbers. This 22 number/symbol/letter alphabet represents twenty two different states of consciousness, whose cosmic energy, essence or relationship seems hard to understand without a deep knowledge and understanding of the Hebrew Tradition.

Unicorn 2000/Aura Light Numerology Chart								
1	2	3	4	5	6	7	8	9
A	B	C	D	E	F	G	H	I
J	K	L	M	N	O	P	Q	R
S	T	U	V	W	X	Y	Z	–

6   6 6   5   = 23 = 5.

TONY COOPER   =11

2   5 7 3   7   9 = 33 = 6.

Vowels Top Line   = Spiritual Purpose   = 5.
Consonants Bottom = Egoic Desire   = 6.
Total   = Overall Self Expression = 11.

Birth Date.. 7 . 4 . 1934 = 10 = 1

DestinyNumber Total = 10 = 1 – Independence etc.

Today we can correlate these 22 images/numbers to help us understand their basic structures. Through the colour combinations we can look past their numbers to discover their essence. The first 22 colour combinations within the Unicorn 2000/ Aura Light Diagnostic System runs with the same flow of these numbers and there is a relationship with the Major Arcana of the Tarot. Coming back to the Pythagorean school of numerology we can see this again focuses within the 00 to 78 colour combinations of the Harmony Diagnostic System.

The universe symbolises the law of the universe....

Each of us is a complete seed of the universe, we are a microcosm of the macrocosmic universe. We are at one with all things and carry the universe within our genes, we therefore possess a universe of possibilities within us, showing that whatever we see within our minds eye exists. Numbers represent universal principles and archetypes through which all things grow and evolve within a cyclic form and they stand for a progression of all that manifests.

Come with me and discover your inner self, your reason for being through the gift of colour, numerology, Tarot and the Kabbalah. By using these magical properties we can analyse personality on many levels as well as relationships with your Self and others, and we can see the body's physical responses to all of this, simply by looking at the colour keys of our Cosmic Code. This Code puts our world into perspective by revealing our patterns of function as well as what some call fate, which we all carry through life.

Let us look and discover how these multi dimensional colour structures which represent combinations of ancient and modern formulas are today having a renaissance of application and presentation. Colour Harmonics can be used to reveal one's state of consciousness and record one's growth and physical well being.

$00+0+1+2+3+4+5+6+7+8+9+10+11+12 = 78$. This sum represents a complete cycle of experiences and also the complete system for The Aura Light diagnostic system. I believe that any system going under or beyond this point are not numerical systems.

The Kabbalah is a philosophical and theosophical system that was originally designed to answer man's eternal question on the true nature of God and the Universe as well as ultimate destiny of mankind. It is based on numerical correspondences between various aspects of human life and the Universal Laws.

Unicorn 2000/Aura Light Colour combinations synthesise with the 78 Tarot Keys to create a system in which other ancient sciences including Numerology, Astrology, Phonics, the Kabbalah and even Aroma Therapy dovetail so neatly into such a beautiful, magical system. Tried and tested through years of research and application, these combinations are what I believe to be The Most Accurate Diagnostic System in the world today. Already the system is used in 20 countries all around the world.

CHAPTER TWENTY

Is Seven a Key to the Cosmic Code?

7....Planetary Cycles.

7....Colours.

7....Octaves of sound.

7....Aspects of the principle elements.

7....Classes and simple elements of minerals.

Everything is connected, for example planets, colours, and sound. Within the creative triangle there is yielded a common factor of 7. These three principles are in intimate union with the four elements, forming seven manifestations of harmony we all encounter on this level of being through 7 colours, 7 sounds, 7 races, 7 principle organs, 7 occult bodies, 7 chakras. It seems there is always a seven factor in any totality of physical manifestation.

Other energetic phenomena are also composed of the seven factor's or potencies within philosophies, such as 7 angels, 7 trumpets, 7 candlesticks with 7 branches, 7 tribes of Abraham, 7 Seals to end this time.

We start at the beginning. As we become colour conscious, followed by the pursuit of colour knowledge, this leads toward colour knowing and this is opening one's self to a greater understanding of COLOUR, the Divine Science.

When one flashes brilliant clear colours reflecting our inner Self and when you are being honest and unafraid and untainted by the opinions of the masses, you have then built a new atom which is free to manifest as the physical form of perfection, which is the real you. This then is allowing you to *show your true colours*, reflecting our Divine Force.

These colours being reflected within one's Aura or the out pouring of one's soul's consciousness, allow you to become the master of your soul and ruler of your thought processes and reveal within the Self a new light, a special radiance which is helping you to find your very own perfect expression of freedom, joy and the special happiness associated with radiant living.

Live, love, and give service to the universe through colour, the great cosmic tuning fork. Colour is the master control of our new race vibration, so go forth reflecting those brilliant facets of the jewel of colour wisdom!

Colour/light...
gives life to every thing that lives,
from plants to people

Alchemical knowledge has been passed down through the ages through many sects, groups, secret societies and certain tribes of Australian, African and American aborigines. Many of them brought with them very ancient and accurate knowledge of the star Sirius, now known as Sirius A, and Sirius B (its orbiting asteroid), which was known to be and now proven to be very dense. Having a five year orbit and said to be our second sun or relay station for cosmic forces, they are supportive energies for our physical and not so physical bodies. They come to us through our Sun to our Solar Plexus, transferring energy patterns which support life itself.

The re-discovery of this very bright star's companion asteroid, unknown to western science up until relatively few years ago, has given cause to look at the ancient legends and verses once again. Is Sirius indeed mankind's seed star, or just a staging post for our cosmic levels of being?

It is said that Lapis Lazuli {Indigo Blue} bottle one, links to the Gods. Knowledge like this has travelled the long road bearing its treasures to be opened right before your very eyes, here today.

Even back from UR and Mesopotamia and as far back as Atlantis and Lumeria, some of these treasures were brought to us by the Sumerians and Chaldian cultures, which cut and polished beautiful gems and crystals, placing them within the foundations of special buildings, as well as setting them into altars. As mentioned within the bible, they showed their recognition of these wonderful mineral and colour links to the earth as well as the solar systems links to the cosmos.

They linked yellow stones to the sun and pearl to the moon, showing they knew that colour was the symbolic language of the cosmos. They then passed this knowledge down through the Hermetic Sciences to Ancient Egypt, and the spiritual alchemy of the adepts from the middle ages. As well this knowledge was part of the mystical wisdom of Israel, through mysteries of the Kabbalah's tree of life.

Aura Light's/Unicorn 2000 Colour Healing Systems incorporates this as well as the Pythagorean science of numbers, together with the energising properties of flower and gem essences blended with specific herb and essential oils. These combinations give a very powerful harmonic structure as a background to each and every colour thus multiplying its natural energy pattern by up to one hundred times or more. Each and every formula imparts profound knowledge and reveals their divine intent.

For the explorer of inner space, colour linked with aroma triggers well hidden modulating patterns proven to be most powerful and giving one access to explore our hidden inner spaces, allowing true spiritual alchemy to take place.

Colour can carry us through time and space, so as to encounter past experiences, even from early childhood. Quite literally to any "Time Slot" within one's life time. Colour then can be a powerful guiding factor for the true seeker or the seeker of the Self. It is said that "The Physical" is just "SPIRIT" condensed and visa versa, spirit is enlightened physical, showing that our lives quest is to bring spiritual energy into form.

Red = MAN = Conscious level of being.
Pale Red = Pink = ENLIGHTENED MAN.
Blue = WOMAN = Sub-conscious. = The force behind the throne of consciousness.
Pale Blue = ENLIGHTENED WOMAN.
Violet = CHILD .= Super Conscious .
Pale Violet = ENLIGHTENED CHILD.

If we look at mankind represented by Red/Blue, before our manifestation on earth we see... Pink/Pale Blue, which links to our present D.N.A./R.N.A. structure.

This is represented by Harmony bottle 61, P/Blue/Pale Pink, which can translate into higher communications of universal love. This I believe is the true blue print {Subconscious Plan} of God given to mankind as a birthright. We are all, in our own way, preparing for a great change in consciousness which will allow us to take part in the quantum leap forward into a new dimension of being.

Our DNA reverses its spiral moving mankind through the Violet Flame of transmutation.

Bottle 62, Pale Violet/Pale Violet:... Linking us with our higher Selves and helping us to co-operate with these higher levels and thus we are reborn into a new structure of being.

Represented by bottle 63, Pale Pink/Pale Blue. This vibration allows us to live within love, not just for love, as we do in whatever form we can find it. But love on the physical level has a way of changing and slipping away, but living within love, it can never be diminished and is forever available to all, especially starting with the love of Self.

Is it possible to give away anything you don't have? ... Then how can you give love to others without loving that being which is you?

Living within universal love requires the quality of enlightened communications with our higher Selves through meditation or prayer.

The bottle 63 shows the enlightened male in its rightful place on the conscious level and the pale blue in the base representing the feminine enlightened sub-conscious. In so many ways we restrict our way forward through the well laid programs from our many pasts, well learnt and embedded deep within one's psyche. We learn that we can open the way just like the old stories say... Open Sesame! We can open the gates and release our own Genie by reprogramming for a positive way forward.

We often have to repeat to ourselves many times and even out loud to evoke this magical power. The password is very simple, but very rarely given. It is:

I give myself permission...

Yes this simple phrase can liberate your thinking, your future, your life. Remember it is only when we change our minds that we change our lives experiences. Giving yourself permission can open the great doors but then you have to go through them to find the new experiences and that great treasure within.

What does this really mean? What sort of restrictions do we place upon ourselves? What do our inbuilt fears stop us from doing or achieving and going forward to?

The seeds of fear were placed within us during our most informative years, mainly within the first seven year cycle. Followed by the second and third seven year cycles within which we believe & re-affirm these original programs by giving them greater expression.

Some of these early programs come from encounters with adults who said, "Who do you think you are?" or similar rebuff's, teaching us on the whole NOT to love or even trust ourselves. We then store these prime fear programs allowing them to surface at any time throughout one's life, not remembering whence this inbuilt fear came from, especially not looking back to a time when we were so small and our parents so big and important.

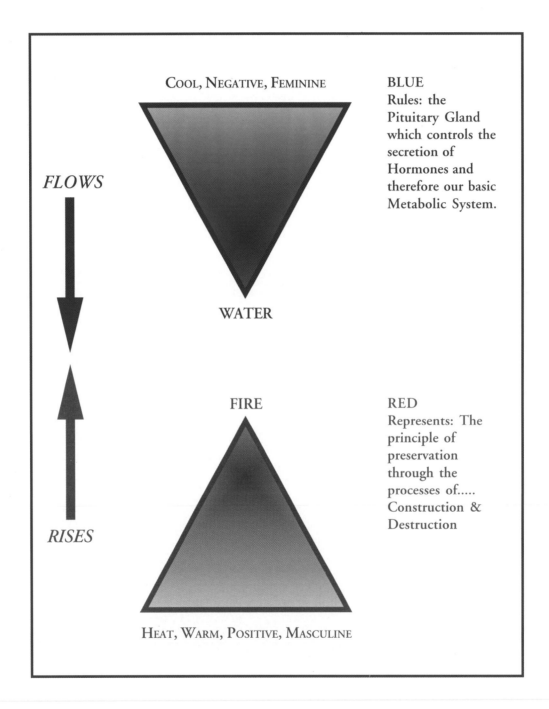

COOL, NEGATIVE, FEMININE

BLUE
Rules: the
Pituitary Gland
which controls the
secretion of
Hormones and
therefore our basic
Metabolic System.

FLOWS

WATER

FIRE

RED
Represents: The
principle of
preservation
through the
processes of.....
Construction &
Destruction

RISES

HEAT, WARM, POSITIVE, MASCULINE

CHAPTER TWENTY-ONE

Love and Fear, the Fulcrum of Our Universe

It has been said many times in many ways that there are only two things in life...
Positive and Negative or Love and Fear, very simplistic, but is it true?

Can living in love come about by simply letting go of fear? This is not a fight but a
simple letting go of fear. Deciding to have the wisdom to control the emotions. In
other words you can decide not to become emotional. Recognising that nobody
makes us emotional, we decide to be emotional and also no one makes us angry but
we decide to be angry.

So you can decide to become the real you and not have to pretend to anyone, even
your Self. Our pretence is usually based on what we believe,{ perceive } not what
other's say we should be. When we can let go of old negative programs, we can go
forward without the subconscious restrictions. **Give yourself permission!**

LOOKING ONCE AGAIN AT....
RED + BLUE = VIOLET and their colour wheel associations .
RED.....Adam....Father. + BLUE ... Eve ... Mother. = VIOLET ....
Being a combination of Red/Blue, Father & Mother, therefore links at childhood to
the parents and one's associations with them.

Violet also says something about the person making their choices as this colour
reflects a time of going within, usually finding that BEING within and forming a
firm relationship with your Self. This introspection triggers a psychic element within
the seeker, such as a good imagination and it is like a child finding imaginary friends
to play with. In the case of children, these friends stay with them until they believe
statements by others of their non-existence.

Violet within first bottle choices gives a good indication that the seeker did not perceive to find the happiness they required within the childhood mainly due to their parents. All these perceived interactions build a very creative person with their psychic gifts returning later in life. Many artists and even managers with very good machinery upstairs in the head, come from this early program, or quality of being.

With this simple base, the archetypes of colour leads you forward to discover the hidden agenda which lies just beneath the surface of specific colours and their inter-relationships ... one to the other. If we maintain this information as we look further into colour, other relationships will be revealed.

CHAPTER TWENTY-TWO

The Platonic Solids

Occurring within the primary levels of being are a higher octave correlation of the five platonic solids. The:

Tetrahedron.

Cube.

Octahedron.

Pentagonal Dodecahedron.

Icosahedron.

There are only 5 three dimensional forms within geometry which are bound by equal plane surfaces all having the exact size and shape. All five are part of our universal spectrum of form, being the keystones to this physical world. Their crystalline perimeters which reflect the Divine Law, allow for an infinite number of ways to manifest into this level of reality. This being the level of primary form where these numeric angular creations formulate into a geometric actualisation and become the basic building blocks allowing mankind to progress into new and even higher vibrational light codings.

This form of manifestation allows mankind to move ever forward into the higher octaves of primary form. These 5 platonic forms have harmonic interaction with the Universe itself, accumulating and reflecting (generating) the complexities of Universal Order. Each acts as a miniature seed blueprint of the inter-patterning of complex relationships within the multi-dimensional universal axis codes of 7 and 32 which relate to the realm of abstract light becoming form. Consider this hidden cosmic light seed code which lies within and beyond matter, as having a resonant correspondence with every colour within one's chakra system.

THE 5 PLATONIC SOLIDS

The Cube
Base Chakra

The Octahedron

The Tetrahedron

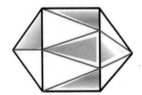

The Icosahedron

The Dodecahedron

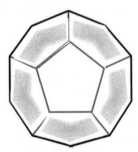

Within these primary forms also lies a correspondence with the full spectrum of numeric and geometric potentialities as they carry a multitude of variations originating from these axis codes. Being highly ordered & multidimensional, the geometry of Cosmic Intelligence carries all its infinite combinations and universal equations. (relationships). These codes or coded patterns give birth to all creation on multidimensional levels of being, attracting and supporting corresponding spectrums of light and being.

The platonic solids are symmetrical, interconnected, inter-dimensional harmonic resonances (vibrations). The colour spectrum equates with the harmonic relationships on a keyboard. This gives an infinite structure and relationship to notes through harmonic structures, creating a resonant transfer of energy. The nature of this energy exchange accords with other potential energy exchanges and the interrelationship of light and colour, numerals and geometric codings. All of which have an affinity with the harmonics, or light dynamics which are essential for the growth of mankind, from the microcosm to the macrocosm. Such organised units constitute a full spectrum of frequencies, giving life and energy to our DNA codes and to the great galaxies far beyond, from the Alpha to the Omega.

Colours, as crystals and platonic solids, are accumulator (Magnetic) generators (Electro). We also receive our life light codes and then generate their particular uniqueness of harmonic frequencies, reflecting their specific vibrational identity. In other words, you participate within the universal electo/magnetic cosmic code.

Each chakra has the basic building blocks of three dimensional geometric pattern which are based on the five platonic solids, that have the following qualities.

1. Cube.... for grounding, stability, earth attunement, physical density.

2. Icosahedron.... for softening one's inner nature, such as rigidness etc., and promotes interaction on personal levels at the same time stimulating creativity.

3. Tetrahedron.... For activating the adrenals and energising, promoting transmutation when change is needed on the physical level as well as within one's consciousness.

4. Octahedron.... For stabilisation, harmonising and integrating on the Physical, Mental & Spiritual levels.

5. Dodecahedron.... For better integration and expression of one's capabilities and plans, in a more creative but systematic way.

6. Octahedron.... Angle of Cheops. Acts like a magnifying glass for electromagnetic focus, which helps our attunement to our blueprint information. The Cheops angles help attunement of the earth's magnetic fields to other levels of consciousness, subconsciousness, collective consciousness, and superconsciousness. Helps telepathic communications as well as astral projection. Also helps enhance sound therapies.

7. Double Tetrahedron.... Helps amplification of one's vibrational essence and reaches the Genetic Code level so as to help restore ones correct patterning. Also helps enhance colour therapies.

* The five interlocking Platonic Solids are connected by the divine proportions within sacred Geometry, being shaped from three basic triangular forms, the triangle, square, and pentagon. Our chakra system utilises all five solids and has an additional two doubles to complete.

* Colour being the language of light, alters the memory substructures of language which affect us on physiological, numerical, biological and cosmological levels of thought attunement and helps to prepare the human mind to embrace the new dimensions of communications now being rediscovered.

This attunement has been made available for the present light workers walking this earth to access the universal coding principles. The language of light can reprogram man's consciousness to participate in the synchronicity of the many dimensions and time zones of one's super consciousness, thereby harmonising the mind and body with one's higher states of consciousness.

The Tree of Life

Viewed from within

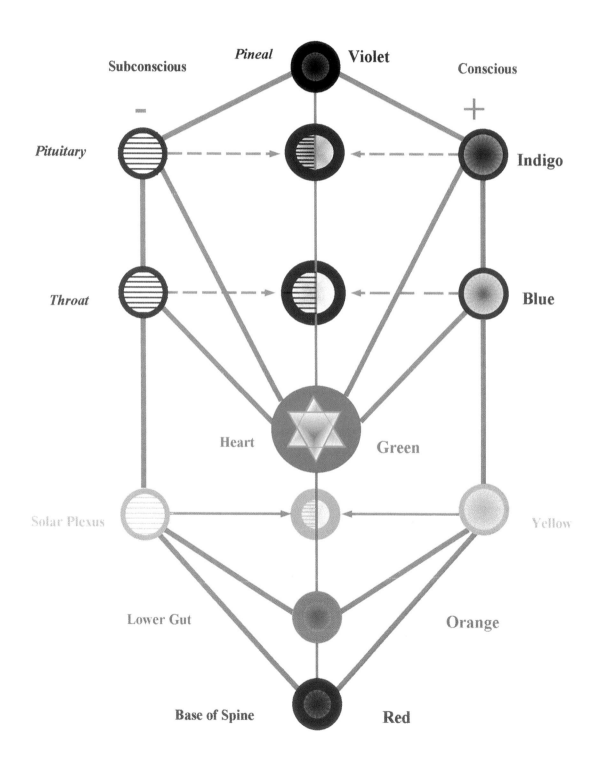

CHAPTER TWENTY-THREE

The Cabalistic Tree of Life

This parallels with the major arcana of the Tarot.

As do our first 23 bottles including no.0.

Colour combinations reveal an invisible intangible reality, something from the inside being revealed to the outer material world, something from the subconscious opening to the conscious level of being. Colour reveals the elusive reality that exists behind the tangible, as well as the strong links between them. At times this hidden reality can show our dreams and potential as well as our psychic essence. It is through the archetypes of the colours themselves and our involvement with them, that we are provided with a new orientation or view of our personal relationships to colour.

This energy opens up new levels of consciousness and understanding within each of our lives. Colour's multi-faceted correspondence with the major divination systems, such as the Tarot, Numerology, Kabbalah and even to a lesser degree the I Ching gives us all a new key to approach and understand the many levels at which colour can relate to us.

This is a system for those who are open to being challenged anew by the mystery and magic of colour and the great wisdom contained within its collective archetype's that dwell within Unicorn 2000/Aura Light's eighty dual tone colour combinations.

The power of these structures of colour combinations never fails to move along it's paths where each one of us finds what each are prepared to discover. Colour opens the questioning soul to facets of its own inner being. The self is dependant on one's own effort and knowledge, but it can transcend and embrace all like minds.

Unicorn 2000/Aura Light's colour Harmony combinations parallel the al chemical images and qualities laid down by and held within the Tarot, Numerology and other divination systems. These images are very important to understand and they help in deciphering the symbolic language of colour which points to the inner spiritual nature of all life and being.

Colour gives us a language of substance that should not be taken subjectively with concrete expression or be taken too literally. We can get carried away with this language, leading us into both the materialised and psychic levels of our beings.

Let us also consider the tree of life as shown on diagram. No.1. Just imagine that you are in fact that image, looking out from within. The + side becoming your right masculine side and therefore the – pillar or side becomes our left and feminine side. Bringing these two sides together merging on a central line, this then represents the chakra system of mankind showing a clear duality of positive and negative, masculine and feminine content to the Chakra's 3, 5 & 6. The others are androgynous within themselves. You can see that the first and second chakras seem to be balanced through the third chakra, but the fifth and sixth chakras have a dual linkage through the Heart or 4th chakra as well as the 7th crown chakra, the head and the heart. It becomes quite clear that the higher chakras have an even stronger linkage to the heart than we would suspect, in comparison with the lower three.

It is said that mankind is spiritual beings of light, and that our essence, our "Spark" resides just behind our breast bone and very close to our heart. The heart chakra is green and is represented within the harmony system by bottle 10.

Green/Green, the wheel of fortune, is bottle 10, and this is in itself very interesting, but when we recognise that green also represents Karma and an opportunity for a new beginning, we can take charge of our life and being, our personal universe. Surely then we can stop the spinning wheel of fortune and get on and off at will and direct our life's course and flow.

True justice I believe, is justice of the heart, well balanced and harmonious. This is where the positive and the negative, male and female meet co-operating on many levels of expression.... from Adam and Eve, Father and Mother, Osiris and Isis, Deep Red and Deep Blue, right through to Pale Red and Pale Blue representing the enlightened aspect of the male and female. Pale Red we call pink, which in turn represents Enlightened Man, The Christ Consciousness, Universal Unconditional Love, all this but still masculine in a finer form. By adding 15 parts of white to blue gives us a beautiful pale blue, which represents Enlightened Woman, The Perfectionist, The Nurturer of the world.

Pink once again has a close connection with the heart as it is an expression of it, therefore whenever we see pink we have an unseen pale green. Remember that pink is really a pale red and the harmonising colour to red is green. The heart is also the pump for the blood (red) and our circulation, co-operative colours indeed. As we can see from diagram, the heart is connected in many ways with the co-operation and harmonising of other chakras.

The cabalistic tree of life shows a central line of contact down directly from the heart touching chakra's 1 and 2, as well as up directly to the 7th chakra and linking to our outer 5 chakras. Both chakra 5 and chakra 6 have secondary links across to both positive and negative pillars, or qualities.

We can also see that chakras 1 & 2 have secondary links to chakra 3, the solar plexus. This is our sun centre which connects the energies of our solar system through the sun, enriching our full physical chakra system, which together with the energy from stars in the outer Cosmos are passed through "Sirius," our second sun and relay station. These energy patterns are passed then to our sun to feed the five higher energy centres above the head.

We can consider the + positive, masculine side as our conscious level of being and the − negative, feminine side as representing our sub-conscious.

IS THE TREE OF LIFE AN ANCIENT BLUEPRINT OF YOU?

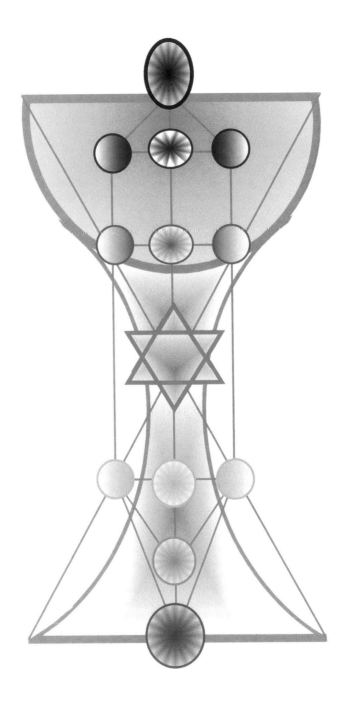

CHAPTER TWENTY-FOUR

Unicorn 2000/Aura Light Colour Harmonics

Self Diagnostic...Self Application...

Holistic self healing systems, for mind, body and spirit.

Recognise colours within your outer world and think about what they really represent, and then perceive how you experience them through your mind's eye. This then allows you to feel their tangible qualities and enables you to organise and re-discover your Self. It is our mission to re-mem-ber (to make whole) our true colours and our personal to planetary links.

As well we can see the universe of hue's that we are, after all we are "hueman" beings.

Our unconscious/subconscious, is the Spirit of Life, which encompasses the life of the universe.

Through colour, let us recognise the inner man, RED and the inner woman, BLUE which together make our inner child, VIOLET. Remember it is from our inner selves that we start the process of healing the self and also know that in the end it is only ourselves that can and has the responsibility to heal oneself. Remember these different levels of self are like medicine and they help restore oneself to harmony and wholeness.

As you take on the responsibility of healing your self, you gain the ability to help others toward the process of self healing. Also the act of weaving your colours together is the first essential step in the process of living your dream, which is to follow your destiny and create your own magic tapestry of life.

Remember it is our unconscious beliefs that form our reality, not our conscious thinking.

The voyage into the inner self, our inner universe, frees us from our self imposed jail of our limited self image.

Through the strength of one's feeling for certain colours we are pulled into understanding their higher meanings for us. By following the feelings that colours evoke, you will find your Spirit Essence.

Unicorn 2000/Aura Light presents a way for each of us to discover our own power, and this is very necessary for our own enlightenment. By following the viable and invaluable colour pathway, spiritual seekers will be lead upon a journey to find themselves. These colour messengers are our true teachers being tangible manifestations of spirit. Colour when perceived with ones own evocative powers, can help us touch our true spirit. The sharing of love is the most fundamental Alchemy of Life, thus the combining of love and wisdom is the essence of compassion.

Unicorn 2000/Aura Light is a way to know yourself more fully, and in so doing embracing a way of self empowerment. By helping one to recognise the power that lies within the self is to create your own reality as well as its manifestation within one's physical life. Colours are but windows through which we can transcend our ego and our thinking minds, for it is from within our inner being that the full manifestation and true power of The Light (which contains all colours) can be made manifest.

Further this enables the HUE-MAN (a being of light and colour), to cast their colours into the physical universe as a beautiful reflection of the rainbow, allowing a manifestation of their true colours, their soul pattern for all to see.

As mentioned Unicorn 2000/Aura Light lies within the ancient traditions of the temples of Egypt and Sumerian Empire and even further back into our distant past, even to Atlantis. Colour, through this journey in time and space, has taken on many facets, but through time its Soul has been mainly forgotten. It is within colour as well as the Rays from which it emanates that the very bones of the universe lie. The most ancient of structures is now being re-energised so as to create "New Man Kind", leading us through this age of "Re New All" into the "Age of Light", when we will be able to give physical expression to our 12 chakra colour modulations, leading us forward toward our not yet forgotten state of enlightenment. This tapestry of inner tracings of colour, weaving in and out of our different levels of consciousness, creates the very fabric of our being.

Unicorn 2000/Aura Light is a modern message of related colour combinations, carrying messages to healers and seekers everywhere.

These colour relationships are but archetypal relationships, leading us into the SACRED RAINBOW DREAM of our subconscious. Within this level of being, we transform not only ourselves but our planet and indeed the Cosmos. Each and every colour has a specific driving force, as does each and every cell and its consciousness. Each cell is then a force within the consciousness of the whole being.

CHAPTER TWENTY-FIVE

Man is the Seed of the Future

Man is the seed of the future enclosed in the pod of the past, set within the Light Aura of thought and thinking which is a refracted reflection of the Light which contains all colour and the subsequent many thousands of hues. This then directs us, through inner sensations, toward direct experiences within life. All colours have qualities of moods and movement which can draw us out or drive us back, or even give us inner stability.

These movements are hard to explain in simple terms, but we all have experienced movements of different kinds which were very real at the time. Through thinking, we realise that colour tells us something of the very nature of the physical.

The colour of the skin not only gives an indication of health but also from what culture that person might come from and so much more. The colour of leaves upon a tree can show its health and the season. We accept all this information colour gives us without a second thought, we trust our senses as a source of knowledge. If we approach colour in an open way we can experience its moods and movements. We must ask the question, is the real nature of colour beyond our physical senses or does it merely awaken those senses to a higher level?

Is colour therefore the gateway to the spirit? Can the spirit through new perceptions of thinking, bridge spirit and matter which have been split apart from birth, but still retain the seed essence?

Through a renewed sense of colour one begins to awaken to the world around us in an exciting new way. The Soul lives and rejoices in colour with a new perception of life bringing a positive response to life and the world around us as it is now a colourful world. As colour speaks to us on all levels, our Soul encourages us to respond to the joy of living.

CHAPTER TWENTY-SIX

Karma

What You Give You Get.

An Opportunity for a New Beginning.

This is the time to be released from the lesson of karma. Karma simply means what you give you get, from this life or from any previous lives on this planet or any other, and also in any dimension.

Mankind is reaching out for that great move forward within this time of the "QUANTUM LEAP". This is a time when the harmonic structure of this dimension reaches a resonance for transmutation, lifting the emerging NEW MAN KIND into this new age.

I like to think of it as The Age of Re-New-All, the coming Age of Light.

Many Souls within manifestation at this time are here to guide and to lead Hue-Mankind across the rainbow bridge of self empowerment through true knowledge and understanding of the real self. These souls are also here to help all mankind to recognise their true line back through time and space, to find their birthright of true being and no longer dwell in the pretence which surrounds us from the cradle to the grave.

We pretend to conform and by so doing give our power away to what we perceive others wish of us,. We respond to the wishes of others such as loved ones, tradition, and the demands of society. We do all that is required of us by acting out the "right" way of being as dictated by social pressure.

As a child we look for approval, acceptance and love from our parents and those nearest and dearest. But in so many cases, our perception rules rather than actualities. In other words, we think that they think this of us. The love and approval that we look for comes from our own state of mind and we are quite prepared to alter even our way of being and our behaviour patterns to earn this approval by pretending to be whatever we think that they want us to be. We do all this to accommodate our perception of other's requirements.

Some of us are quite prepared to be good, even perfect, to gain mother's approval. This state is often aimed for if one or the other parent is a perfectionist. It seems to be true that when we don't receive the portion of love within a relationship we try for the next best thing, approval.

So many of us are still looking for approval from parents even when they are not still living within this vibrational frequency. We hear people say, I just know that dad would be so pleased to know that I have done so well, to have bought this beautiful house ...and the like.

Even within a good loving relationship we still alter our behavioural patterns to accommodate, what we think our loving partner would approve of, or what we think they think should happen next, or simply what they would like!

We have a need to please, but to please who or what? It seems nothing more than our own perceptions.

As we travel through the adventure of life we go from parents to school where we would like to be accepted by a certain range of other children or group, what do we find our self doing? Yes we just want to be what we think these other children would like us to be, even though no one actually says what they want of you. Maybe they are too busy pretending to be what they think you want of them.

Now that we are all grown up, have we grown out of pretending to be, or are we in so many ways still trying to get those approvals?

When it comes time to choose a good relationship and someone to share your life with, are we still pretending to be, or do we realise that like attracts like. If one person is pretending within a budding relationship ten to one the other is also. One needs to stand firm and come forward in truth and to be unafraid of being your self, for real people attract real people into their relationships which can then last a life time.

It is time to start practising and developing into that real wonderful you. Explore within your self and use the magical tool of colour to find what has lain hidden for so long.

The sharing of love is the most fundamental Alchemy of life.

Love can bring out the magic of the mind, helping us to trust the process of life and living. The principle of love has the power to enter each and every heart and therefore every home especially where discord or sorrow dwell. Love can share its radiance and joy and this is the very essence of peace. Once having accomplished its mission, it returns to the sender multiplied. This process is the key to higher consciousness. We need to love the things that we do, together with everything that we have created in our daily lives.

Remember we have the choice of loving or fearing every thing or situation, we just need to adjust our way of perceiving or being and decide to become the actor within our lives, not the re-actor.

When we learn to interpret life through colour, we can find the elusive essence of truth, because love's essence is an unchanging immutable law which cannot lie. Colour is the elevator lifting us through our higher levels or phases of consciousness and expression without any loss of continuity, for colour is capable of interpreting these different planes of being for us. Many ancients have written of love and it is said that *Love* is the secret of life which was inscribed upon the Sphinx. It was also written near Mount Sinai. Other writings say that Love is the perfume of the soul, and Love is the spirit of a sparkling star, and that the torch of life is fed by the oil of love.

Whilst the sharing of love is the most fundamental Alchemy of Life, the combination of love and wisdom is the essence of compassion. Pink translates our different loving relationships, deep pink indicates a more physical level of love, a paler pink links us to a more enlightened unconditional love. At times we interact with conditional or conditioned love which equates with a fear of loving, giving us a little yellow (fear) within the pink and this is shown as apricot or rose pink.

Colour is the outpouring of the Logos/Light, the great tuning fork. Each colour has its very own frequency of vibrations, linking to the manifestation of the Rays and the planes they exist upon through which the physical is made manifest.

CHAPTER TWENTY-SEVEN

Colour and Music

Each colour has its own musical note forever singing in cosmic rhythm with its own supportive Ray deep within the Logos and playing its cosmic tune. Every colour also has a special close relationship with specific aromas, herb, flower, gem, and importantly, a numerical quality. When some or all of these various frequencies are put together with a particular colour something quite amazing happens. Instead of just adding one value to another they multiply each others energy, giving not just a colour but a harmonic structure to use in one's life experiences, within home, business and within society.

This powerful combination helps to balance your physical expression of health bringing power to the chakra system on all levels and also, increasing power and production on every level of endeavour.

Through transferring the basic energetic patterns of the universe, of which there are said to be 14 atomic patterns or harmonic structures within the mineral kingdom here on earth, we converse with the Devas, which in Sanskrit means being's of light. The Devas can co-operate by interconnecting different levels or fields of consciousness, which have evolved from the other Kingdoms such as nature spirits (Fairies), elementals and Angels.

Our human race has inadvertently created, for want of a better word Devas as something, at times, negative. Large groups, cities, countries, collections of people create a collective consciousness of combined thought forms, which can be a wonderful power for good, but more likely in a time of negative focus, not so good. As a human race we must realise and wake up to the power of like minded people creating "combined thought forms" with the possibility of passing their focused dreams on to the rest of the human race through the co-operation of the Devas.

As we move into this Aquarian Age, the age of re-new-all, energy and thought will take form from the growing numbers of light seekers and through the collective and focused power of the Enlightened who will be networking around the world helping to heal this planet and all of mankind upon it.

To heal this planet and mankind, we must first release the cause and not try and relieve only the symptoms, which are but the physical manifestation of the cause.

Each level of being has its own consciousness and individual rate of growth. Right through from below the humble cellular levels to the physical levels and on to the sub-conscious and the conscious, out past the Astral body levels to one's spiritual and soul bodies right up through the 12 chakras. This consciousness then continues up through the rainbow serpent, the energy flow that connects all levels and that which is our direct link to the Creator.

We can follow this path with the steps of colour vibrations, which emanate from a point of origin within the centre of the Cosmos and spread into a band of magical frequencies reaching each step of our evolution both on a physical and conscious level.

Just open your imagination and dream the great dream of crossing the Rainbow Bridge.

CHAPTER TWENTY-EIGHT

Messengers in Bottles.
Why Colour, Oil, and Water?

Colour in itself transfers associated Rays together with each specific colour vibrational frequency, which then influences both physical and subtle levels of being.

Oils main influences are achieved through the transference and or alignment to their associated Rays and Planetary energies. These vibrational preparations influence the subtle levels such as the Meridians, Chakra and other subtle bodies, thus affecting the physical itself.

Within the Harmony bottles, the oil takes the higher portion within each bottle. This represents the "Conscious" level of being and therefore carries frequencies and patterns because each colour and hue is being primed with very specific vibrational patterns to be generated to the physical body via the body's many inner and outer energy systems. Through the chakra centres these energies and patterns are directed to our physical cellular level, reaching those cells levels of consciousness, renewing energy patterns or grid consciousness. Every cell carries within it, a complete set of blue prints or patterns which are your unique coding. If you can change enough of these cells consciousness, this will have a direct effect upon your consciousness. It is from these levels of being that many of our physical imbalances become disease which is then promoted and transferred into the physical body.

Water influences all levels via its electro-magnetic memory function, facilitating the transfer of a very wide range of vibrational frequencies from flower, gem, shell and stellar origins with integrity.

Water has been proven recently, but known for many years, to have an electro magnetic memory. Laboratory trials that were recently run in the U.K. showed that a

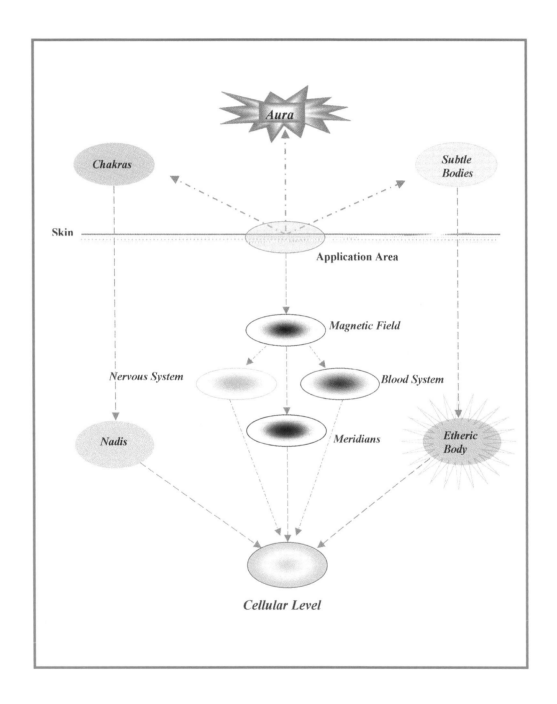

COLOUR THE COSMIC CODE

given drug worked well on its subjects. Then after being watered down many times until there was no physical trace of the drug, the water carrying the drugs patterns within its memory still worked well on its subjects.

The lower "Subconscious" portion of each Harmony bottle has a distilled spring water base, which is capable of holding projected memory patterns with integrity for very long periods. We have found that certain spring waters have a far better memory than others. It has been found that water put through a triple filter with reverse osmosis, cancels any memory that the water had, to a point where it is dead and decays rapidly, unable to hold the required projected memory patterns.

As we know the human body is made up of 65% water, having its own electro-magnetic memory. The interaction between these bodies of water is a powerful medium for harmonic responses between each other, helping to create harmony of the physical body.

Every colour within the lower portion of the Harmony bottles is energised with some 22 levels of energy, transferred from Gems, Shellfish, Flowers, Herbs, plus Essential Oils and projected frequencies of certain musical notes and three dimensional patterns including the main platonic solids. All have a similar frequency base to the colour, creating a harmonic structure supporting each particular visible colour. Together with the specific frequency of each colour being projected into the water carrying each colour, integrity is given to each bottle even if for some reason it loses its colour. (People Take Colour)

A harmonic structure is a series of energy patterns built upon and co-operating with each other, magnifying or multiplying each other's energy, giving a very powerful tool. Western civilisations categorises creation into states of Matter, Solid, Liquid, Gas, and Radiance. But in Eastern terms their classification is of, Earth, Water, Air, Fire, to which the Chinese have added the element of Wood.

EARTH...The stabilising form, without which there could be no physical form.
FIRE...... Gives movement and flow to static form, and promotes dispersal.

AIR........Transcends these lower levels and raises energies to a higher form.

WOOD.. Is the synthesis of pre-existing elemental forms bringing about an entirely new species of being.

Throughout history there has always been a recorded correspondence between metal, planets, and colours. It is interesting to consider ...WHY these correlate.

IRON is identified with Mars, the Greek God Aries and the colour RED.

GOLD identifies with the SUN, The Egyptian God RA, colour orange/Yellow. Gold's spectral rays are situated within the yellow/gold zones of the spectrum. Masculine.

SILVER identifies with the MOON, and with the colour white, which represents the totality of colour. Feminine. Is also identified with THOTH who is said to regulate times and seasons.... also the Moon.

There are many other correlation's and correspondences with colour and metals. Some bring out strange phenomenon within their spectral sequences which compete, compensate or cancel each other. All have different relationships with each other.

Element	Wood	Fire	Earth	Metal	Water
Organ	Liver	Heart	Spleen	Lungs	Kidneys

Through recent studies it has been confirmed that our electro-magnetic state is manifest as an etheric grid system of a crystalline lattice structure, hexagram in nature. This is a primary geometric pattern which links with the holographic level of The Rays.

Thoughts and feelings are ELECTRICAL in nature, held together with MAGNETISM which faces at 90 deg. involving direction and pattern. In many ways this is like Einstein's theory of relativity.

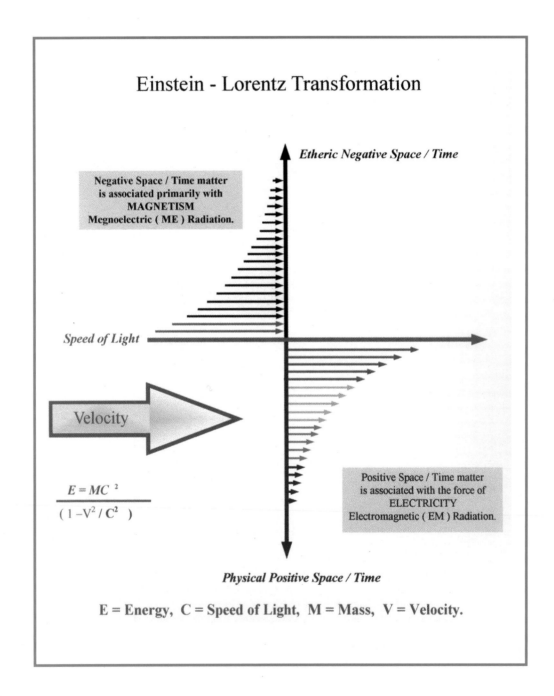

Einstein - Lorentz Transformation

Etheric Negative Space / Time

Negative Space / Time matter
is associated primarily with
MAGNETISM
Megnoelectric (ME) Radiation.

Speed of Light

Velocity

$$\frac{E = MC^{2}}{(1 - V^2 / C^2 \ )}$$

Positive Space / Time matter
is associated with the force of
ELECTRICITY
Electromagnetic (EM) Radiation.

Physical Positive Space / Time

E = Energy, C = Speed of Light, M = Mass, V = Velocity.

The physical space/time universe...

Particles which make up the physical ATOM are electrically charged as positive, negative or neutral.
The electro-magnetic theory predicts that all particles have north and south poles. Our universe is based on living systems, biological systems which take simple raw materials such as food and organise it into complex macromolecular structures such as protein, D.N.A., collagen etc. This living system displays properties of negative entropy. It seems that LIFEFORCE is associated with Negative/Magnetic principles. When we look at the death of the physical form, the life form vacates the physical moving back into the cosmos. The remaining unoccupied shell returns to its raw constituent.

Consider the body as being a self organising holographic energy template, demonstrating negative and positive properties.

Within the physical space/time universe......

It is said that:

❖ *Positive space/time matter exists only at velocities less than the speed of light.*

❖ *Negative space/time matter moves faster than the speed of light.*

CHAPTER TWENTY-NINE

Life is a Journey of Discovery. Colour is Your Guide.

Life is a journey of discovery.... self discovery and finding out who and what you are, even if at times, reluctantly. At other times, we follow the edicts passed on to us by many other learned souls, who prompted us to: KNOW THY SELF.

We wander the many highways and byways of life finding many sign posts that tell us where we really don't want to go. There are oh so many directing us the wrong ways from within and without of our own society and in many different languages.

Quite often we find refuge and respite down some little quiet lane where no one bothers us allowing us to just let life pass us by quietly and not wake us up to the fact that this is the main event .... there is no re-run.

We must realise that we need to seize the day and make it work for us and realise that we need to make it happen, what ever it is and to just do something, anything. If we can just get our minds into gear, throwing off our mind locks thus allowing access to our imagination and thought processes, we can recognise the well disguised links to our thinking/feeling processes. After all, our thoughts and feelings are both electrical and chemical in nature with their patterning held together magnetically. When we have been reared on a diet of lies, half truths, fears, prejudices and contradictions, its no wonder that any sensitive soul wants to get "lost" down that quiet lane or back water.

Now is the time of the "seeding" of a new wisdom and a recognition of what is, not what yoke society has put around our shoulders.

You are free to have any thought you wish, for you are in charge. We have thought every moment of our lives, its time to consider what we are doing with all these

———

thoughts, remembering that clear thoughts get clear results, muddled thoughts get muddled results, and no thoughts get no results.

A great number of mankind have no positive thought projection and therefore find no positive thought form to move into.

I think I am, Therefore I am .... this is this the key to our wellbeing and being well, being successful and being happy. Energy follows thought and then manifestation follows energy. Therefore nothing can manifest without thought first. Be creative with your thoughts, dare to be different!

What is your dream thought for your particular future? Remember that No thoughts equals No results.

The universe out there is rather like a fantastic super-market, just waiting for your "choice" so that it can be made manifest for you. The clearer you can make your dream the easier the universe can supply. We must then think now of what we want to do with our thoughts, having the power to think every moment of one's life, we should appreciate that we have decided to be exactly where we are right now.

See what power we have and understand that we just need to control our thinking. It is said that up to 90% of our thinking is based on our emotional responses thus showing the programmed response of our feelings to each and every thought. With every feeling we produce a chemical and hormonal response within the body, giving a good chance of over or under production and so creating a balance or imbalance within the physical body.

The variation between all or some of these elements can bring the body into dis-ease which we relate to as an illness. Consider then toxic thoughts & genetic thought patterns unwittingly produce various toxins that can manifest within various parts of the body.

Your dream is yours to create, so follow your passion, follow what ever excites you. Its time now to take off those mind locks and to let your imaginations fly free, get into that positive thoughts focus and hold it. Do it now!!

Positive thoughts are great but what gives them their power is "Expectancy", that is what you really expect, this is the real power house, just as the old fashioned word faith has a very similar base. Know that we can only be positive through clear thinking, remembering that in life we only ever get in the end just what we expect to get.

Our thought habits govern our eating habits, our exercise habits, our working or not working habits as well as our relationship habits. Through your inner communications, are you giving yourself the right messages?

Are you saying "I am sick of this and sick of that," and your body replies "O.K. be sick," or are you saying "I just love my work" and getting the reply "O.K. enjoy".

Re-programming for better living...

Let us consider what programs we hold that are in some cases life threatening.......
Realising that our "PROGRAMS" are perpetuated through our interaction and reaction with others.
Let's ask ourselves....WHY ?....

Why do we accept beliefs as truths? It seems that if we believe in anything for a long time, we believe it to be the truth, but in reality they are only things believed in for a long time!

When we personally don't know, why then do we believe others views of things. Its a good time to remember that POWER for some is getting others to agree with their view, their reality and their "Truth".

Why is a habit a program?
Why is a trait a program?

Why are many hereditary or genetic problems a program?
Why are our eating habits programmes?
Why therefore is one's weight and size a program?
Why is a phobia a programme?
Why is conditional love a programme?

Why do we carry so many programs and where did they all come from?

What forms our perception our beliefs?

Is it the data which we compare with our inner programs handed down or more accurately taught to us as small children?

Is it our country's programs, our societies, our religion or culture, or could it be our schools, work and even our family, our mother, lover and brothers, or is it simply all the above mentioned and much, much more.?

We are all told how we should act, therefore we view the World as a whole and either respond or react through love or fear. We are told what we should consider being good or bad, as well as what behaviour is considered good or bad within your society. In fact we are programmed (taught) to judge and consider others, decide who or what they are and just as importantly whether they conform to "our" set programs.

What are all these programs?

Did you know that in a lot of ways we are rather like a computer which can accept many levels of programs, some very basic, others very sophisticated and very well hidden. It's within the structures of inner learning or programming we base our translation of reality. These programs that connect our thinking to our feeling are often incorrect in so many ways. An example might be the type of message that is received from say a parent who dislikes and fears horses or dogs or even certain foods. These prejudices or fears are often passed on to our children and maybe on to further generations.

Our programs are assimilated into our living everyday life through what we call attitudes, which we use to translate the World to our inner selves. All these links are learnt patterns and can be un-learnt through understanding your inner motivations. We can even limit or change our formed behaviour patterns that show a need to get approval (get along with) others..

Time to take your self to the pictures...you will soon learn that picturing is a very powerful aid to achievement within sporting activities, healing or even at work. **Learn to imagine a perfect result thus cancelling out bad results.**

Just put your self in the picture. Today, right now let's get visualising. By putting a thought in a particular direction you will be empowering yourself and starting to complete the picture. This is much better than any blueprint, just imagine it complete, finished and perfect, what ever it is. A very good example on a physical level for instance is a frozen shoulder. Remembering that some thought process, conscious or sub-conscious put it there, now your thinking can take it away. The first step is to recognise the problem and own it. How often do we have problems that we don't want to recognise? Consider that our drinking and smoking or our love of cream cakes or chocolate can all be addictions.

Lets now take time to spend on us, ourselves, you and me. It will help to play a relaxing piece of music that you personally like to create the right atmosphere and vibrations to achieve.

Right from the start EXPECT the perfect result that you desire as this brings the power to make your positive thought and visualisation manifest.

So what has all this to do with colour?

Are we not a living cosmic code? Or are we colour coded hue-man beings of light and colour, whose basic colour code is our chakra colours which are a reflection of the rainbow, right through from our base chakra of red to our crown chakra of violet. Enlightened man has been likened to the living rainbow, reflecting all colours in this level of being.

The Hue-man aura is an energy field around the body that has colour, movement and flow. You can light the universal livingness together with energy and electromagnetic radiation, characterised as colour.

Colour is used to diagnose disharmony within the body and this is what we call illness. We positively respond to colour, our colour preferences are subconscious keys to buried emotions and our relationships to others and to ourselves.

Light and colour influences interrelate with our moods and feelings. Red is the longest wavelength and lowest frequency which refracts the least. Violet is the shortest wavelength and longest frequency with the greatest refraction. To illustrate, a carrot absorbs short wave light and reflects longer wavelengths, which we perceive as orange.

Our original DNA/RNA code being represented as Pale blue/Pale pink, is a lot more enlightened than the physical manifestation of you and I. Remember red for the male and blue for the female and that red represents the conscious level of being and blue the sub-conscious.

Red/masculine/Sol.   Blue/Feminine/Lunar.
Bottle 61
Pale Blue/Pale Pink = enlightened Female/enlightened Male
= Eros/Logos = The Chalice.

The Unicorn

The time has come
For the Unicorn to return to earth
To blaze the way
For man to accomplish his spiritual rebirth.

Look to the heavens
For the time is surely near
Look in wonder,
Mankind has nothing to fear.

The Unicorn comes once again
To cleanse our planet's peril
And with the coming,
A New Age will be herald.

The Unicorn returns to prepare us
For our true purpose,
He comes with inspiration,
To nuture, to guide us.

The Unicorn is to replenish and restore
Our earth to a place of grace,
Where body, mind and soul
Can aspire to an exalted state.

Your Unicorn will soon be here
To rekindle your sacred fire,
To unveil the great heights obtained
Upon fulfilment of the Creator's desire

The Unicorn is coming,
Expect their return,
Open your hearts and minds
This time its your turn.

Shiralee Cooper, 1989.

CHAPTER 30

The Great Conspiracy

Conspiracy is the first manifestation of intelligent life and conspiracy is the normal continuation of normal politics by normal means. Where there is no limit to power there is no limit to conspiracy. Power is getting others to accept only your reality. The double cross is very often the basis to man as is deception (pretence). Disguise and group action also have a long evolutionary history. OUR HISTORY.

Nations have no permanent allies, only permanent interests.
People have no permanent allies, only permanent interests.
Real wealth consists of things, ideas that work. Money consists of tickets, symbols, and numbers that can be stored in banks, computers and ledgers.
Therefore money is not real wealth, it consists only of tickets of exchange for the REAL WEALTH. This is all part of the Grand Illusion that we call REALITY.

COLOUR challenges the grand illusion opening the cosmic doors to inner realities. Is it now time for you to discover your real wealth, the real you.

The information within this book is not meant to be the last word on colour but a sign post creating awareness and understanding and showing the way forward.

This information and advice is not meant to replace that of your doctors but simply to show a different way of viewing things. **I view colour as complementary to other therapies and other systems of healing, not alternative.**

This book includes information which is, in part, practical in nature and the content can be easily digested by any interested person. It also presents a more sophisticated blue print and outline for the professional's use and application.

COLOUR THE COSMIC CODE

We have then gone forward to an area of more complexity for the Visionary, providing ground breaking philosophical and conceptual foundations which encourage access to the Cosmic Inter-dimensional spectrum of networks and advanced grid-works connecting many energy levels from the sub atomic Microcosm, to the Mega dimensional Macrocosm.

This is the time to facilitate assimilation of deeper levels of understanding and development by mankind to support the great leap forward, the quantum leap.

Its not just the path we choose.....

But the way we walk that Path.

So let us all "walk our talk".

The Language of colour expresses cosmological constants which support both human and higher evolutionary thought forms.

Colour is the language of light that alters the memory substructures of language which affect us on physiological, numerical, biological and cosmological levels of thought attunement. Colour helps to prepare the human mind to embrace the new dimensions of communication that are now being rediscovered.

In the main mankind has not used the Language of Colour, because humanity has remained under the power of fallen Illuminaries, aligning themselves to duality, black and white. Losing their conceptual ability to work with other Polychromatic (Colour Coded) vibrational realities.

The language of light & colour alters the memory and substructures of our inner cosmic language, affecting our physiological, neurological, biochemical and cosmological levels of thought and attunement to facilitate the preparation of the human mind to enjoy the exciting new levels and dimensions of communications, which were originally seeded here for use of this planets light workers who are now walking this plane.

The Cosmic Code

The Cosmic Code has been given as a gift to mankind. With wisdom and intelligence seeded within, the order in which these keys are presented is an exact numerical sequence. We can only advance physically through consciously advancing using our thought forms which are in essence the creative connection to the super grids of the cosmic creative source. It is here where the essence of the Light enfolds the cosmic codes once again to be seeded within this time through colour, sound, numbers, and crystalline geometric structures. Through this cosmic language our consciousness is activated to communicate on many new levels, which then can become immersed within our own levels of reality.

The opening of the higher mind clears and clarifies the many channels to the higher Universal Wisdom of the Seven Seals, Seven colours, Seven chakras, This wisdom reveals that as we experience all colour, we experience the light, helping us to find our" mastership" and rightful place within the Cosmos. The keys are encoded within colour and other harmonic structures, seeding them with the Living Light split into a new spectrum carrying its hidden alphabet to be released and realised within this dimension, spelling out mankind's collective birthright. These keys now being made manifest are preparing mankind for the Quantum Leap forward, bringing changes effecting every level of intelligence upon and within this planet, giving an opportunity for mankind to collectively move into a new system of creation and a new consciousness within the light.

Since the keys have been given together with their teachings to within many varied disciplines, thus making them therefore difficult to be understood by all, the complexity of each key will not be fully recognised at this time and will take various levels of understanding to recognise the totality of their encoded planetary intelligence.

The Cosmic Code was created to shape a new creation within the full spectrum of light and Octaves of sound etc., all creating a regenerative harmonic power of Biocoupling expressed through colour combinations, and each colours geometric blueprint. These energised combinations are to be used directly onto the body thus re-coding it back to the Light allowing it to consciously experience the direct power of the sacred language and projected thought forms that it holds within.

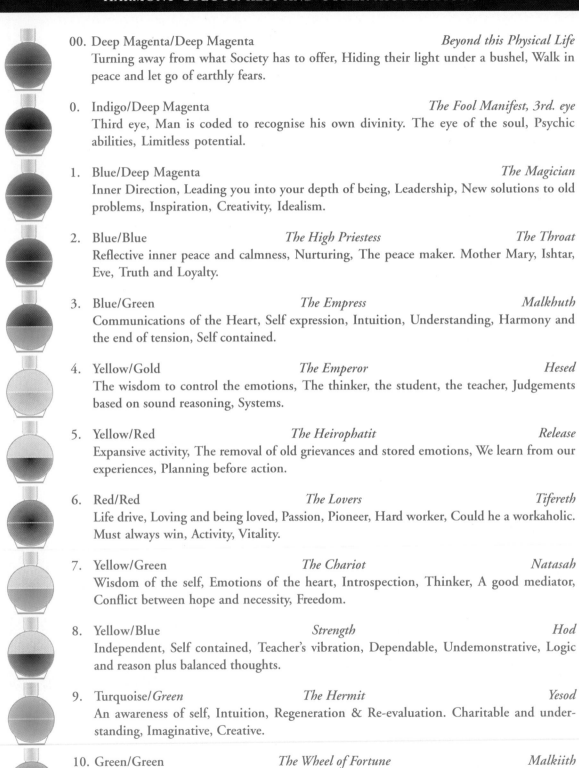

00. Deep Magenta/Deep Magenta   *Beyond this Physical Life*
Turning away from what Society has to offer, Hiding their light under a bushel, Walk in peace and let go of earthly fears.

0. Indigo/Deep Magenta   *The Fool Manifest, 3rd. eye*
Third eye, Man is coded to recognise his own divinity. The eye of the soul, Psychic abilities, Limitless potential.

1. Blue/Deep Magenta   *The Magician*
Inner Direction, Leading you into your depth of being, Leadership, New solutions to old problems, Inspiration, Creativity, Idealism.

2. Blue/Blue   *The High Priestess*   *The Throat*
Reflective inner peace and calmness, Nurturing, The peace maker. Mother Mary, Ishtar, Eve, Truth and Loyalty.

3. Blue/Green   *The Empress*   *Malkhuth*
Communications of the Heart, Self expression, Intuition, Understanding, Harmony and the end of tension, Self contained.

4. Yellow/Gold   *The Emperor*   *Hesed*
The wisdom to control the emotions, The thinker, the student, the teacher, Judgements based on sound reasoning, Systems.

5. Yellow/Red   *The Heirophatit*   *Release*
Expansive activity, The removal of old grievances and stored emotions, We learn from our experiences, Planning before action.

6. Red/Red   *The Lovers*   *Tifereth*
Life drive, Loving and being loved, Passion, Pioneer, Hard worker, Could he a workaholic. Must always win, Activity, Vitality.

7. Yellow/Green   *The Chariot*   *Natasah*
Wisdom of the self, Emotions of the heart, Introspection, Thinker, A good mediator, Conflict between hope and necessity, Freedom.

8. Yellow/Blue   *Strength*   *Hod*
Independent, Self contained, Teacher's vibration, Dependable, Undemonstrative, Logic and reason plus balanced thoughts.

9. Turquoise/*Green*   *The Hermit*   *Yesod*
An awareness of self, Intuition, Regeneration & Re-evaluation. Charitable and understanding, Imaginative, Creative.

10. Green/Green   *The Wheel of Fortune*   *Malkiith*
Heart Chakra, Karma, Brings Growth, New Beginnings, New Direction, Luck, A turn for the better. New relationships.

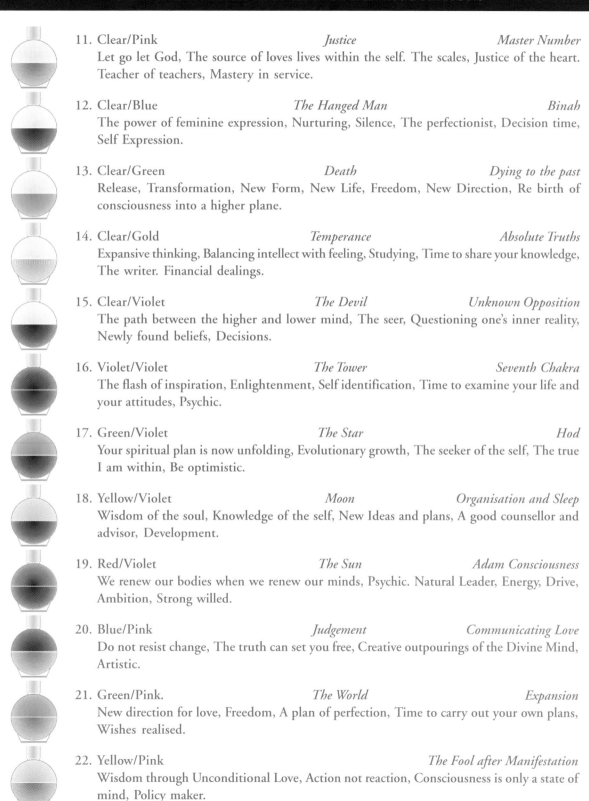

11. Clear/Pink   *Justice*   *Master Number*
Let go let God, The source of loves lives within the self. The scales, Justice of the heart. Teacher of teachers, Mastery in service.

12. Clear/Blue   *The Hanged Man*   *Binah*
The power of feminine expression, Nurturing, Silence, The perfectionist, Decision time, Self Expression.

13. Clear/Green   *Death*   *Dying to the past*
Release, Transformation, New Form, New Life, Freedom, New Direction, Re birth of consciousness into a higher plane.

14. Clear/Gold   *Temperance*   *Absolute Truths*
Expansive thinking, Balancing intellect with feeling, Studying, Time to share your knowledge, The writer. Financial dealings.

15. Clear/Violet   *The Devil*   *Unknown Opposition*
The path between the higher and lower mind, The seer, Questioning one's inner reality, Newly found beliefs, Decisions.

16. Violet/Violet   *The Tower*   *Seventh Chakra*
The flash of inspiration, Enlightenment, Self identification, Time to examine your life and your attitudes, Psychic.

17. Green/Violet   *The Star*   *Hod*
Your spiritual plan is now unfolding, Evolutionary growth, The seeker of the self, The true I am within, Be optimistic.

18. Yellow/Violet   *Moon*   *Organisation and Sleep*
Wisdom of the soul, Knowledge of the self, New Ideas and plans, A good counsellor and advisor, Development.

19. Red/Violet   *The Sun*   *Adam Consciousness*
We renew our bodies when we renew our minds, Psychic. Natural Leader, Energy, Drive, Ambition, Strong willed.

20. Blue/Pink   *Judgement*   *Communicating Love*
Do not resist change, The truth can set you free, Creative outpourings of the Divine Mind, Artistic.

21. Green/Pink.   *The World*   *Expansion*
New direction for love, Freedom, A plan of perfection, Time to carry out your own plans, Wishes realised.

22. Yellow/Pink   *The Fool after Manifestation*
Wisdom through Unconditional Love, Action not reaction, Consciousness is only a state of mind, Policy maker.

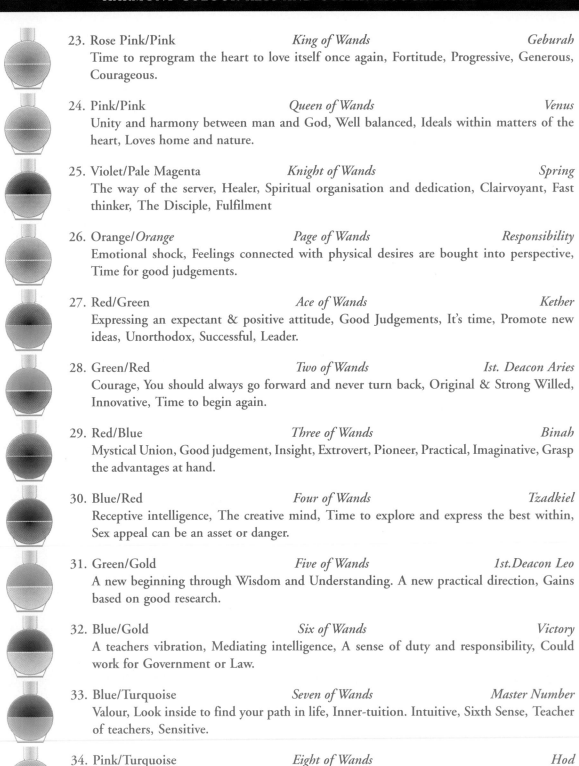

23. Rose Pink/Pink   *King of Wands*   *Geburah*
Time to reprogram the heart to love itself once again, Fortitude, Progressive, Generous, Courageous.

24. Pink/Pink   *Queen of Wands*   *Venus*
Unity and harmony between man and God, Well balanced, Ideals within matters of the heart, Loves home and nature.

25. Violet/Pale Magenta   *Knight of Wands*   *Spring*
The way of the server, Healer, Spiritual organisation and dedication, Clairvoyant, Fast thinker, The Disciple, Fulfilment

26. Orange/*Orange*   *Page of Wands*   *Responsibility*
Emotional shock, Feelings connected with physical desires are bought into perspective, Time for good judgements.

27. Red/Green   *Ace of Wands*   *Kether*
Expressing an expectant & positive attitude, Good Judgements, It's time, Promote new ideas, Unorthodox, Successful, Leader.

28. Green/Red   *Two of Wands*   *Ist. Deacon Aries*
Courage, You should always go forward and never turn back, Original & Strong Willed, Innovative, Time to begin again.

29. Red/Blue   *Three of Wands*   *Binah*
Mystical Union, Good judgement, Insight, Extrovert, Pioneer, Practical, Imaginative, Grasp the advantages at hand.

30. Blue/Red   *Four of Wands*   *Tzadkiel*
Receptive intelligence, The creative mind, Time to explore and express the best within, Sex appeal can be an asset or danger.

31. Green/Gold   *Five of Wands*   *1st.Deacon Leo*
A new beginning through Wisdom and Understanding. A new practical direction, Gains based on good research.

32. Blue/Gold   *Six of Wands*   *Victory*
A teachers vibration, Mediating intelligence, A sense of duty and responsibility, Could work for Government or Law.

33. Blue/Turquoise   *Seven of Wands*   *Master Number*
Valour, Look inside to find your path in life, Inner-tuition. Intuitive, Sixth Sense, Teacher of teachers, Sensitive.

34. Pink/Turquoise   *Eight of Wands*   *Hod*
Loving relationships, Honesty, Discriminating, Introspective, A determined approach to life, Completion comes after travel.

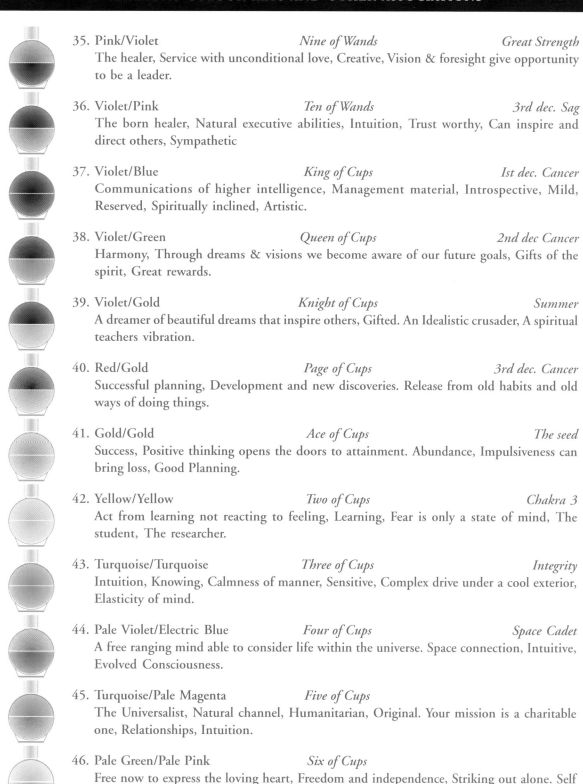

35. Pink/Violet   *Nine of Wands*   *Great Strength*
The healer, Service with unconditional love, Creative, Vision & foresight give opportunity to be a leader.

36. Violet/Pink   *Ten of Wands*   *3rd dec. Sag*
The born healer, Natural executive abilities, Intuition, Trust worthy, Can inspire and direct others, Sympathetic

37. Violet/Blue   *King of Cups*   *Ist dec. Cancer*
Communications of higher intelligence, Management material, Introspective, Mild, Reserved, Spiritually inclined, Artistic.

38. Violet/Green   *Queen of Cups*   *2nd dec Cancer*
Harmony, Through dreams & visions we become aware of our future goals, Gifts of the spirit, Great rewards.

39. Violet/Gold   *Knight of Cups*   *Summer*
A dreamer of beautiful dreams that inspire others, Gifted. An Idealistic crusader, A spiritual teachers vibration.

40. Red/Gold   *Page of Cups*   *3rd dec. Cancer*
Successful planning, Development and new discoveries. Release from old habits and old ways of doing things.

41. Gold/Gold   *Ace of Cups*   *The seed*
Success, Positive thinking opens the doors to attainment. Abundance, Impulsiveness can bring loss, Good Planning.

42. Yellow/Yellow   *Two of Cups*   *Chakra 3*
Act from learning not reacting to feeling, Learning, Fear is only a state of mind, The student, The researcher.

43. Turquoise/Turquoise   *Three of Cups*   *Integrity*
Intuition, Knowing, Calmness of manner, Sensitive, Complex drive under a cool exterior, Elasticity of mind.

44. Pale Violet/Electric Blue   *Four of Cups*   *Space Cadet*
A free ranging mind able to consider life within the universe. Space connection, Intuitive, Evolved Consciousness.

45. Turquoise/Pale Magenta   *Five of Cups*
The Universalist, Natural channel, Humanitarian, Original. Your mission is a charitable one, Relationships, Intuition.

46. Pale Green/Pale Pink   *Six of Cups*
Free now to express the loving heart, Freedom and independence, Striking out alone. Self Discovery.

47. Indigo/Yellow.   *Seven of Cups.*   *2nd dec. Scorpio.*
E.S.P, Truth and Trust, High standards, Left & Right Brain, Depth of feelings, Self knowledge, Writer, Painter, Visionary.

48. Violet/Clear   *Eight Of Cups*   *1st. dec. Pisces.*
Time of decisions, Draw down the Light and proceed with care, If it feels right do it, Seeking your path. Purity.

49. Turquoise/Violet   *Nine of Cups*   *2nd. Dec. Pisces.*
Elasticity of mind and spirit, Natural Channel, Multi gifted, Complex, Imaginative, Original, Communications of the heart.

50. Pale Blue/Pale Blue   *Ten of Cups*   *Isis/Eve*
Enlightened woman, The nurturing of mankind, Meditation, The mind is conscious of many worlds, Internalised search.

51. Pale Yellow/Pale Yellow   *King of Swords*   *Wisdom*
True justice, The liberated mind using its full resources to find the Truth. Rewards for clear positive thinking. Assimilation.

52. Pale Pink/Pale Pink   *Queen of Swords*   *Love*
The will of the Higher self, Mankind's highest ideals, Acting and not reacting. Unconditional Love is not an Ivory Tower.

53. Pale Green/Pale Green   *Knight of Swords*
The enlightened heart, The way of truth and light, Regeneration. New beginnings with a fresh sense of purpose, Open hearted.

54. Clear/Clear   *Page of Swords*   *Willpower*
Decision time, Inspiration, Liberation, Expansive consciousness, The power of the Light, Revelation, Go, the path is now clear.

55. Green/Clear   *Ace of Swords*   *Freedom*
The will of God (The Light) is the way, Renewal, Re-creation. Purification of the heart, May the *Light* illuminate your plans.

56. Green/Pale Green   *Two of Swords*   *Karma*
The good Samaritan, Unselfish thought and actions, Completion, New beginnings be it way of life, mental attitude or religion.

57. Pale Turquoise/Pale Turquoise   *Three of Swords*
Self awareness, A deep still pool of reflection, Exacting, Planetary to personal activity, Sensitive, Intellectual.

58. Pale Pink/Pale Yellow   *Four of Swords*
Love and Wisdom, Discrimination through love, The loving purpose of the Divine Mind, A desire for knowledge & wisdom.

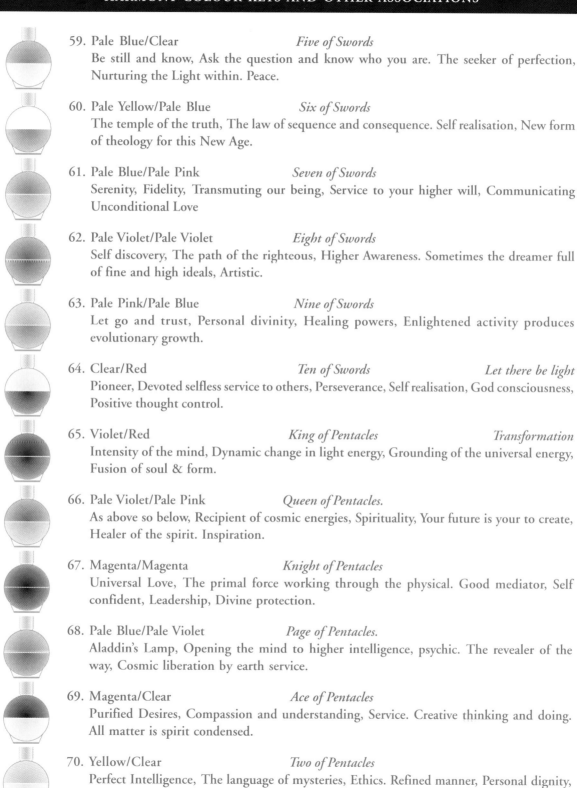

59. Pale Blue/Clear   *Five of Swords*

Be still and know, Ask the question and know who you are. The seeker of perfection, Nurturing the Light within. Peace.

60. Pale Yellow/Pale Blue   *Six of Swords*

The temple of the truth, The law of sequence and consequence. Self realisation, New form of theology for this New Age.

61. Pale Blue/Pale Pink   *Seven of Swords*

Serenity, Fidelity, Transmuting our being, Service to your higher will, Communicating Unconditional Love

62. Pale Violet/Pale Violet   *Eight of Swords*

Self discovery, The path of the righteous, Higher Awareness. Sometimes the dreamer full of fine and high ideals, Artistic.

63. Pale Pink/Pale Blue   *Nine of Swords*

Let go and trust, Personal divinity, Healing powers, Enlightened activity produces evolutionary growth.

64. Clear/Red   *Ten of Swords*   *Let there be light*

Pioneer, Devoted selfless service to others, Perseverance, Self realisation, God consciousness, Positive thought control.

65. Violet/Red   *King of Pentacles*   *Transformation*

Intensity of the mind, Dynamic change in light energy, Grounding of the universal energy, Fusion of soul & form.

66. Pale Violet/Pale Pink   *Queen of Pentacles.*

As above so below, Recipient of cosmic energies, Spirituality, Your future is your to create, Healer of the spirit. Inspiration.

67. Magenta/Magenta   *Knight of Pentacles*

Universal Love, The primal force working through the physical. Good mediator, Self confident, Leadership, Divine protection.

68. Pale Blue/Pale Violet   *Page of Pentacles.*

Aladdin's Lamp, Opening the mind to higher intelligence, psychic. The revealer of the way, Cosmic liberation by earth service.

69. Magenta/Clear   *Ace of Pentacles*

Purified Desires, Compassion and understanding, Service. Creative thinking and doing. All matter is spirit condensed.

70. Yellow/Clear   *Two of Pentacles*

Perfect Intelligence, The language of mysteries, Ethics. Refined manner, Personal dignity, Faith in the future.

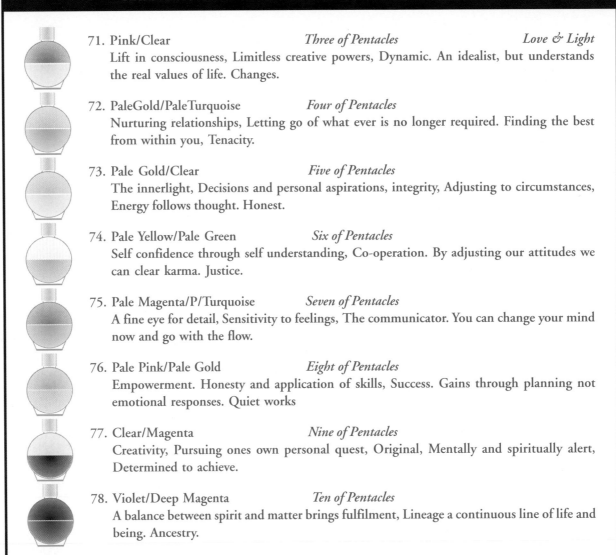

71. Pink/Clear   *Three of Pentacles*   *Love & Light*
Lift in consciousness, Limitless creative powers, Dynamic. An idealist, but understands the real values of life. Changes.

72. PaleGold/PaleTurquoise   *Four of Pentacles*
Nurturing relationships, Letting go of what ever is no longer required. Finding the best from within you, Tenacity.

73. Pale Gold/Clear   *Five of Pentacles*
The innerlight, Decisions and personal aspirations, integrity, Adjusting to circumstances, Energy follows thought. Honest.

74. Pale Yellow/Pale Green   *Six of Pentacles*
Self confidence through self understanding, Co-operation. By adjusting our attitudes we can clear karma. Justice.

75. Pale Magenta/P/Turquoise   *Seven of Pentacles*
A fine eye for detail, Sensitivity to feelings, The communicator. You can change your mind now and go with the flow.

76. Pale Pink/Pale Gold   *Eight of Pentacles*
Empowerment. Honesty and application of skills, Success. Gains through planning not emotional responses. Quiet works

77. Clear/Magenta   *Nine of Pentacles*
Creativity, Pursuing ones own personal quest, Original, Mentally and spiritually alert, Determined to achieve.

78. Violet/Deep Magenta   *Ten of Pentacles*
A balance between spirit and matter brings fulfilment, Lineage a continuous line of life and being. Ancestry.

These eighty combinations complete our diagnostic/Divination Systems as they mirror and align to many other systems including The Tarot and the Kabbalah. Harmony Bottles are available in 35 ml. Glass bottles or 50 ml. Plastic.